FREED TO LIVE

Also by the author:

Healing Adventure
Trial by Fire
Study Adventure in Trial by Fire
Jesus, All in All (with workbook included)
Dayspring
Healing Devotions
The Transforming Power of God

FREED TO LIVE

Anne S. White

with Appendix by
The Rev. Dr. Alfred L. Salt, D.Min.
M.A., B.D., A.M.P. (Harvard Business School)

A book to challenge others to accept this freedom through Scriptural, balanced teaching and the witness of some of many thousands who have been FREED TO LIVE as the Lord has used Victorious Ministry Through Christ to fulfill His Promises in Luke 4:18-19:

"to set the captives free, to give sight to the blind and to open prison doors."

Copyright © 1989 by Anne S. White.

First Edition 1989 in the United States.

Victorious Ministry Through Christ, Inc.
P.O. Box 1804, Winter Park, Florida 32790.

All rights reserved. No part of this publication may be reproduced or transmitted by any means or in any form without the written permission of the author or the publisher.

Scripture quotations, unless stated otherwise, are from the Revised Standard Version, copyright 1946 and 1952 by the National Council of the Churches of Christ, U.S.A. (Division of Christian Education).

ISBN 0-9605178-3-9
Library of Congress Catalog Card Number 89-90273

Typesetting by Thoburn Press, Tyler, Texas

Printed in the United States of America

DEDICATION

This book is gratefully dedicated to my Heavenly Father, my Savior and Healer Jesus Christ, and to the Holy Spirit who guides and empowers my life.

To my loving husband — now in Glory — and to my daughter and son, Maryanna and Richard, for their loving, prayerful support of the VMTC Ministry as a "third child" in my life.

To the loving, faithful Board of Directors and Team Members of Victorious Ministry Through Christ (in USA and other countries) who have heard and fulfilled the Lord's call to extend this Scriptural Ministry to bless those to whom they minister and to deepen the work of the Holy Spirit in the renewal of the Church.

CONTENTS

Acknowledgements ix
Foreword xi
Introduction xv
  1. Overcome by Life — or by the Power of the Spirit! 1
  2. The Drama of Redemption 7
  3. From a "Walking Wounded" to a "Walking Miracle" 17
  4. God Is Faithful 25
  5. Trust in the Lord 35
  6. Praise Changes Us 43
  7. Termites in the House of Life 51
  8. Forgiveness Is a Beauty Treatment 61
  9. The Christian Family 69
10. The Church as the Bride of Christ 81

APPENDIX *by the Rev. Dr. Alfred L. Salt, D. Min., M.A., B.D.*
Introduction: The Nature and Scope of VMTC
               Prayer Counseling 91
  1. The Ministry Defined 93
  2. The Ministry: Basic Principles 95

ACKNOWLEDGEMENTS

My grateful thanks go not only to those few mentioned in the Foreword but also to others of the eleven Clergy Members of the ecumenical Board of Directors of Victorious Ministry Through Christ—USA. Without the very sacrificial commitment of each one of these men of God, this Ministry could never have grown and survived such heavy "Spiritual Warfare."

Additionally, my heart rejoices in the dedicated commitment of the many Clergy and Lay Leaders abroad whom God has called over the years to transplant to their Churches this Victorious Ministry Through Christ—whether in Australia, Canada, Finland, Sweden and more recently in Pakistan. The Ministry could not have spread without the commitment of many hundreds of faithful Team Members who have served the Lord over the years—lovingly, cheerfully and without remuneration—in the intensive VMTC Clergy Schools of Prayer Counseling—for His Glory!

This manuscript has been enriched by the addition of the Appendix which gives a fine explanation of the nature and scope of VMTC Prayer Counseling. The Rev. Dr. Alfred L. Salt, VMTC's Vice President, has kindly shared this portion from his dissertation for his D. Min. Degree.

FOREWORD

For several years, the Lord has been laying on my heart the need to write a new book—but a very busy travelling schedule has prevented my intended efforts from becoming a reality! One night I prayed: "Lord, I really have no desire to write another book—because I haven't time to do it; and besides, proof-reading manuscripts is wearisome work! But, if this is something You really want me to do, You'll have to anoint me with Your message. And, please enable Kathy and me to flow in the Spirit so that the manuscript can be completed before I leave for Singapore in two months!" After that, I began preparing to go to bed as it was 10 o'clock and I had a busy day planned ahead at the office.

Suddenly, I knew that I had to go to the "Florida Room" where I usually keep my "Quiet Time" each morning. There I have always experienced God's Peace—from the very day I moved the furniture into that glass enclosed room which looks out on the miniature garden the Lord had guided me to landscape. (I had moved favorite shrubs, ferns and plants from the big half-acre garden of my previous home so that I would not be homesick in the new setting which had looked very bare when I originally bought the house.)

Two hours later, my yellow pad had recorded on its pages the beginning of the message that the Lord wanted me to write for the first chapter! The next day, Kathy (our new secretary) typed it into the Word Processor and so began my prayerful commitment to finish work on the manuscript in between trips to Atlanta, New Mexico, New Orleans, Singapore and Sweden! Each night as I prayed, the Lord's message flowed smoothly through me—and each morning, Kathy typed and printed it out for me to take home and proof-read that night. It has been a joy to work closely with Kathy Hummel as her constructive comments and Christian perspective have made her far more valuable than an ordinary typist! The Lord answered my prayer as we "flowed in the Spirit" joyously—even when she had to "tame the computer" which sometimes tried "to glitch" on us. I was also blessed by the much-needed editorial help of several members of our Board of Directors: the Rev. Drs. Clifford Horvath, Kenneth Sprinkle and Alfred Salt, the Revs. Vernon Stoop and William Westlund. They carefully read this manuscript and added their perspectives to the teachings as well as some of their personal experiences.

Their comments were most encouraging! Gems from my rector's anointed sermons have often flowed unconsciously into this text. While on their vacation, the Rev. and Mrs. Roger Miller wrote detailed, helpful suggestions which made me rejoice as they strengthened the clarity of the original version. Also, our new Associate Central Coordinator and his wife, the Rev. and Mrs. Bruce Urich, became part of the Lord's answer to my prayer as they cheerfully took over the exacting burden of careful proof-reading and tedious checking of Scripture references—even volunteering to check the final manuscript as well as the earlier rough draft! My prayer partner, Loretta Moore, read it as we travelled the thousands of miles to Singapore—and two of her stories are included in the text. I am grateful to the many "walking miracles" who have allowed me to use their moving witnesses to help encourage others.

My prayer is that this teaching book with real life stories from our VMTC Prayer Counseling Ministry (as well as from my personal life) will help readers to grow in awareness of the surety of God's Wisdom, Faithfulness and Love. My intention in using the stories is to help others to see

Foreword

where VMTC Prayer Counseling (as a valid, Scriptural, balanced, Spirit-led Ministry) helps today "to set captives free, to give sight to the blind and to open prison doors"—so that the committed Christian can truly become FREED TO LIVE in the Power of the Holy Spirit! This counseling has proven to be a valuable tool of ministry within the Body of Christ, the Church. It helps combat the dangerous influences of secular humanism, occultism and the New Age Movement as well as the sad effects of so-called "charismatic humanism."

May FREED TO LIVE help readers to see and experience the Reality of the Victory of Calvary and the Power of the Holy Spirit today, as they build their lives on the teaching and authority of God's Word. May this message "whet the appetites" of those who need to experience the very real and lasting blessings received in VMTC Prayer Counseling as a ministry which helps to bring renewal in the Church by strengthening its clergy and lay leadership to stand fast in today's ever-increasing "Spiritual Warfare!"

ANNE S. WHITE, *President*
Victorious Ministry Through Christ—USA
and VMTC—International Coordinator

P.O. Box 1804
Winter Park, Florida 32790

INTRODUCTION

In 1981, after several years of full-time pastoring, both my wife and I had been very wounded—even by some of the well-intentioned ministry we had received. We were at the end of our rope when we were introduced to Victorious Ministry Through Christ by a friend who had been ministered to by Anne S. White and a trained pastor during a Clergy School of Prayer Counseling. In desperation, we traveled 700 miles to attend our first School and received such release and healing that we determined to make this training an integral part of our ministry.

In the ensuing years, we have continued to be blessed through VMTC—Anne's seven books, the Retreats and Clergy Schools of Prayer Counseling as well as the privilege of ministering in depth to other pastors, not only in the U.S.A. but also in other countries. As we have used this ministry in our pastorate, we have seen countless lives changed and people "freed to live"—not unto themselves, but in total commitment to Jesus Christ!

THE REV. LONNIE D. SHIELDS, *Senior Pastor*
New Life Christian Fellowship
Grand Rapids, Michigan, U.S.A.

ONE

OVERCOME BY LIFE —OR BY THE POWER OF THE SPIRIT!

*T*he signs of our times literally scream with headlines: "OVERCOME BY LIFE!" Physically, mentally, economically, emotionally and spiritually the world seems to be headed on a collision course labelled "Bankruptcy"—from which many people fear there is no return! The threat of nuclear annihilation hangs like a huge mushroom cloud while men cry, " 'Peace, peace,' when there is no peace" (Jer. 6:14). Rather, each day seems to bring further fulfillment of the Scripture: "And Jesus answered them: 'Take heed that no one leads you astray. For many will come in my name, saying "I am the Christ," and they will lead many astray. And you will hear of wars and rumors of wars; see that you are not alarmed; for this must take place, but the end is not yet. For nation will rise against nation, and kingdom against kingdom, and there will be famines and earthquakes in various places: all this is but the beginning of the sufferings' " (Matt. 24:4-8).

It is helpful, in contrast, for us to read what the Apostle John wrote: "For this is the love of God that we keep His commandments and His commandments are not grievous.

For whatsoever is born of God overcomes the world, and this is the victory that overcomes the world, even our faith" (I John 5:3-4). We are called to be overcomers by the Power of the Spirit—not to be overcome by the powers of darkness at work in today's world! We are called to show forth the Love of God in a world that literally breathes violence and hate! We are called to be "aglow with the Spirit" (Romans 12:11)—not quenching God's Power in our lives with faithless fears. Indeed, Paul wrote to Timothy words that we need to heed today: "For God did not give us a spirit of timidity, but a spirit of power and love and self-control"—not of fear but of a sound mind (II Tim. 1:7)!

In place of living life-styles of depression, bitterness, self-pity, loneliness, and lack of purpose, God has predestined us *in Christ* to fulfill as His sons and daughters the purposes that He has had for us from before the foundation of the world (Eph. 1:4-5). Instead of succumbing to confusion and powerlessness, our Heavenly Father calls us to know that He is not "the author of confusion but of peace" (I Cor. 14:33). Instead of allowing sick emotions to cause (in all too many cases) sick bodies, He calls us to yield ourselves spiritually, mentally, emotionally, and physically to Jesus' healing Power flowing through His Body the Church today. Instead of allowing broken relationships to cripple us and those we love, God's Will is for us to be made whole—to be healed in spirit, soul and body.

Today, everyone seems either *to have a problem* or *to be a problem*! For a man, the fierce competition to make a success in his vocation causes tensions that can lead to high blood pressure, a stroke, or a heart attack. The uncertainties in the economic world, the high cost of living, the cut-throat styles of business competition, the dangers of the present political situation, the fear of nuclear explosion—all of these combine to make a man feel "overcome by life" unless he has the Reality of the Power of the Holy Spirit to guide and sustain him! Jesus promised the twelve disciples that He would send the Holy Spirit to guide them into the Truth. In the maze of today's humanism with its conflicting calls and false promises, a man needs the wisdom of God to find the way for himself and for his family — the Way to true fulfillment of his purpose in life through Jesus Christ!

Especially for us women, Jesus' answer to life is *vital*! We live in the center of a wheel of relationships — with husband, children, parents, in-laws, neighbors, teachers, employers and countless friends. Attitudes toward any of these people affect our other relationships. If we awaken depressed in mind and take it out on the children, it will probably be reflected later on Johnny's report card. The husband who goes off to work without a cheerful, loving embrace from his wife is not going to be as well prepared for the boss' reprimand or the contract that failed to come through on time. The critical word that slips from our tongue about a neighbor's child can be the beginning of a neighborhood feud — even involving the husbands' and children's relationships with each other. The quick retort on the telephone to a demanding mother-in-law will not ease the family tension and may cause lasting "buried wounds of the spirit!" How can we, as women, carry the accusations, the frustrations, the fears that assail us and not be emotional wrecks? If we try to escape through television or reading novels, the stark realities of our own lives will still be there to face us when the program or chapter is finished. If we make cigarettes our crutches, the doctors warn us that we are surely writing our own tickets for cancer or heart disease, or even harming our children — thus adding to our list of guilts! If we escape through nibbling and over-eating, we hate ourselves — because the added pounds soon make us look and feel bulkier and our clothes no longer fit! Problems seem to breed *more* problems! A day of rest is never a reality.

Also, the percentage of women in the working force is ever increasing as every decade brings periods of transition. Challenges to live on one salary within today's cost of living have forced many women to become "bread-winners." Some women choose to continue a career after marriage and others work outside their homes because of the loneliness of an "empty nest." In all these situations, couples should remember that a good marriage is just like a savings account: it's only good as long as the interest is kept up.

Even more complicated is the life of the single person who has survived divorce (or death of a spouse) and is trying to re-stabilize his (or her) situation. Being a "single parent" is the hardest of all challenges — especially when it is necessary to be the "bread-winner" also. As the percentage of singles grows, their plight becomes worsened by limited opportunities for adult fellowship. Usually being a parent and "bringing home the bacon" consumes all their energies. For them, loneliness is a *real* problem.

You may be saying to yourself even at this moment: "But, you don't understand the horrendous financial problems of our family." *Or*, "You don't know my husband's terrible anger." *Or*, "You don't realize how my mother-in-law subtly tears me down." *Or*, "You can't imagine how my children exasperate me." *Or*, "You haven't tried to live next to my neighbor." *Or*, "You don't know how difficult my employer is!"

There is One who does know — One who has promised "to be with *you* always, even to the end of time" (Matt. 28:20). Jesus wants you NOW to come to Him — all you who are "weary and heavy laden" so that He can refresh you! He wants to heal you of the jealousy and bitterness, the fear of rejection and long buried resentments, the low self-esteem and fear of confrontation, the self-pity and guilt that corrode your life — poisoning you in spirit, crippling your will, churning your emotions and destroying your peace of mind. No wonder that your body reacts to all of this in *dis*-ease! You want God to change *others* — but He wants to begin with *you*! As you allow Jesus to become fully the Lord of your life, in this new relationship you will begin to live in His strength, not your own. You can say with Paul: "I can do all things in him who strengthens me" (Phil. 4:13). You can begin to claim with him: "Thanks be to God who gives us the victory through our Lord Jesus Christ" (I Cor. 15:57). You will come to know the reality of the Old Testament promise: "The joy of the Lord is your strength" (Neh. 8:10).

As a child of God there is no hurt or affliction, no evil that can break us—unless we give up the battle! We have Jesus' authority—but if we capitulate and throw in the towel, we mis-use our God-given freedom of will. Strangely enough, the more the Israelites were abused by Pharaoh, the more they multiplied during their sojourn in Egypt. Someone once said that our responsibility is to "respond to *His* ability." As my rector challenged us recently: "Don't pull the plug! Out of great turmoil, God often brings something better—but we have to hang in there until He brings His healing, transforming Power into our situation." The life of an overcomer is tested in battle—our God reigns over the circumstances that seem to us so bleak and hopeless and dreary. We grow our spiritual muscles through these battles and we need to praise God in the midst of them that *He is still God!*

"Persevering in prayer" is a Scriptural but not always popular teaching today. Abraham waited 100 years for Isaac, the child of promise; and Paul spent years after his dramatic conversion experience searching Scripture and "growing in the Lord"—maturing in Christ—although he had long been a Jewish rabbi. Our culture, however, demands *instant everything*: from "instant oatmeal" to "instant divorce"—to say nothing of "instant success!" In the original Greek, the present imperative of Matthew 7:7 would be, "Ask, and keep on asking; seek, and keep on seeking; knock, and keep on knocking." In a recent sermon, my rector pointed out that a baby chicken gives us a practical example "peck, and keep on pecking": when the chick finds his protected environment becoming too cramped, he begins to peck his way out of the shell and he keeps on pecking until he is free to move in a new way of life. How often we humans stop too short of a victory because we will not keep on praying—prevailing in prayer! The enemy will try to discourage us from this Scriptural attitude of persevering in prayer by his false insinuations, such as: "Don't you know that you're going to fail?" or "What makes you think that you can do this?" or "What will people think of you?" or "You're making a fool of yourself."

Satan tempted Elijah with discouragement trying to make him give up on being serious concerning the things of God. Elijah cried out, "It is enough O Lord, take my life" (I Kings 19:4). Our personal enemy tries to tempt us to despair and give in to temptations that constantly beset us in our Christian walk. We need to hold on to the practical wisdom in James 4:7 where we read: "Submit yourselves therefore to God. Resist the devil and he will flee from you."

Someone once said: "God will fix a fix to fix you — and if you unfix the fix before He fixes you, He will fix another fix to fix you." It is often our Heavenly Father's way of training us in spiritual discipline — because He knows our need to learn *to trust totally in Him*! If we dodge (or try to escape from) a necessary testing in life, God may bring us back into the same kind of situation until at last we learn the lesson that He has been trying to teach us. He loves us too much not to prune us when we need this so that we can bear more fruit!

Let us begin by laying aside all of our old preconceived concepts so that we can seek a clear, fresh understanding of Scripture as Truth. Let us look at the Bible as "the drama of redemption" so that you can build your life on the firm foundation of its Truth — not on the shifting sands of modern secular humanism or any past unscriptural confusion concerning God's Will and Purposes — for you and for His world. Let us seek to know the promises of His Word as the basis for becoming "an overcomer" in the Power of His Holy Spirit. Knowing *about* God and *knowing* God are totally different concepts! Jesus calls you and me to be "more than conquerors" in today's turmoil (Rom. 8:37). Will you seek His Victory in your life through this study of His Word as you come to understand it as "the Drama of Redemption"?

TWO

THE DRAMA OF REDEMPTION

*A*s omnipotent God, our Heavenly Father created us in His own image, giving us the freedom to choose whether we will live our lives in unity with His Purposes—or whether we will live in rebellion and try to "play God" in our own lives as well as in the lives of others. Because Satan clearly rebelled against God's divine authority and fell from heaven as a result of his pride and violence, he tries to influence us to follow his wicked rebellious choices (Is. 14:12-15).

Scripture tells us here and elsewhere that Satan (also called Lucifer) was created "blameless" as one of the most beautiful of the angels—but his pride set him up for his down-fall because he plotted rebellion against God Himself! Satan's ambition was to sit on God's throne and to make himself "like the Most High." But, as he sinned and was filled with violence, he was cast "as a profane thing from the mountain of God"; and one third of the angels fell with him! In Ezekiel 28:17, we read: "Your heart was proud because of your beauty; you corrupted your wisdom for the sake of your splendor." Does this warn us? What about violence, pride and the lust for splendor in our lives today? If Satan tempted Jesus in the wilderness three times, we can be sure that he will tempt us today—and often in the same ways! The first temptation for Jesus to turn stones into bread involved "Appetite." The second temptation to give Jesus authority over the kingdoms of the world involved "Ambition." The third one to cast Himself from the pinnacle of the temple involved "Applause." Jesus resisted this strategy and rebuked Satan by quoting the Word of God decisively (Luke 4:1-13). So the devil departed from Him until a more opportune time! (In JESUS, ALL IN ALL, Chapter VIII, I wrote a more complete explanation of "Spiritual Warfare.") How can we follow our Master who was tempted even as we are but did not sin?

Our ancestors, Adam and Eve, fell because they succumbed to the temptation to eat of the forbidden fruit and disobeyed God in the Garden of Eden. So, the serpent (Satan) tempts us today to make rebellious choices, contrary to our Heavenly Father's Will for us as His sons and daughters. Our sinful nature (inherited from Adam and Eve down through generations) can only be redeemed when we are "born again" into the Kingdom of God and the Lordship of His Christ. At that time, our sin nature is broken as the Holy Spirit enters and resides in our spirits—so that we can really call Jesus "Lord" in the depth of our beings. "No one can say 'Jesus is Lord!' except by the Holy Spirit" (I Cor. 12:3). This "new birth" experience deals with our sin nature —but we can still sin as evidenced by the many Scriptures on "confession of sin" found in the Epistles to the Churches. In John 3:5-6, Jesus is recorded as saying, "Truly, truly . . . unless one is born of water and the Spirit, he cannot enter the Kingdom of God. That which is born of the flesh is flesh, and that which is born of the Spirit is spirit." So, it is obvious that regeneration is a vital and necessary step for each one of us. This is totally opposed to the teachings of today's humanism where we are tempted to believe that we can "play God." But in a very real sense we Christian believers can say: "We have been saved, we are being saved, we will be saved!"

Although salvation begins when we accept Jesus Christ as Lord and Savior, *the continuing process of changing our lives to be conformed to His image* is a lifetime's work (Rom. 8:29)! We are justified by faith in Him but we are sanctified by His Spirit *abiding in us* to bear the fruit of the Spirit. Jesus gave us the key when He said: *"Abide in me,* and I in you. As the branch cannot bear fruit by itself, unless it abides in the vine, neither can you unless you abide in me . . . He who abides in me, and I in him, he it is that bears much fruit, for apart from me you can do nothing" (John 15:4-5, italics mine). Someone once wisely wrote: "Justification can come in a minute (as one accepts Jesus Christ to be Lord and Savior) but sanctification is a life-time's work!" Even as an orange tree takes time to grow and bear fruit, so do we when we live in fruit-bearing union with Jesus as our King and Master. God has called each of us from before the foundation of the world in Christ Jesus to be His sons and daughters (Eph. 1:4-6). We are called to *be* His Will—not just to *do* His Will! How easy it is to forget *being* in our eagerness to serve Him with our many "doings."

As we praise our Heavenly Father for who He is, we can give thanks that He has given us that most precious of all gifts—the gift of His Son! Through His perfect obedience to the Father even unto death in the most painful and degrading of ways, Jesus has redeemed what Adam lost in the Fall! Jesus has given us the Holy Spirit to make possible for us this salvation (wholeness) experience. As the Holy Spirit glorifies Jesus, so Jesus glorifies the Father! The Holy Spirit abiding in our spirits will enable us to glorify both our Heavenly Father and Jesus. The Holy Spirit responds to our decision to allow Him to operate in our lives—but He does not take away our freedom of will.

Jesus *in us* can win the Victory in "Spiritual Warfare" to which all of us are subject once we really decide to follow

Him. We have long been taught that we have a personal Savior—*but most people in the Church today do not realize that they have a personal enemy, the same one that Jesus had!* Satan is always trying to deceive us or falsely accuse us as he would like to rob us of the Victory that Jesus won for us at Calvary. Scripture tells us: "The reason the Son of God appeared was to destroy the works of the devil" (I John 3:8). No wonder Satan did his best to destroy Jesus—but the Resurrection proved Satan to be a defeated foe. Praise God!

In Hebrews 2:14-15 and 17-18, we read: "Since therefore the children share in flesh and blood, he himself likewise partook of the same nature, that through death he might destroy him who has the power of death, that is the devil and deliver all those who through fear of death were subject to lifelong bondage. . . . Therefore he had to be made like his brethren in every respect, so that he might become a merciful and faithful high priest in the service of God, to make expiation for the sins of the people. For because he himself has suffered and been tempted, he is able to help those who are tempted."

We are given a clear warning that we are not to be like the Israelites who grumbled in their disobedience after God had brought them safely out of Egypt—and thus they "were unable to enter because of unbelief." That generation had to die off—they could not enter the Promised Land! Perhaps when we are going through suffering in life, we need to read a little farther about Jesus in this important Epistle to the Hebrews until we come to verses 8-9 in chapter 5: "Although he was a Son, he learned obedience through what he suffered; and being made perfect he became the source of eternal salvation to all who obey him. . . ." Jesus is the source of our salvation for dying—but He is also the source of our deliverance and "wholeness for living!" Like the disciples at Pentecost, you and I can receive the empowering of the Holy Spirit even as was prophesied by the prophet Joel (2:28-32) and confirmed by their changed lives following their first dramatic experience in the Upper Room (Acts 2:1-4)! After that, the Peter who had once denied Jesus preached so eloquently that 3,000 people were converted in one sermon! We read ". . . many wonders and signs were done through the apostles" (vs. 43b). "And the Lord added to their number day by day those who were being saved" (vs. 47b). The early Christian Church grew strong in spite of cruel persecution by sadistic Roman emperors who wanted to wipe out the worship of Jesus so that they themselves could be worshipped as gods by their people.

In today's world, the humanists seek to wipe out the worship of Jesus so that man can usurp God's place—as in New Age Philosophies and cults that emphasize the glorification (deification) of man! We Christians are called to unite against these forces of evil—to be overcomers in the power of the Lord and in the strength of His might through the Holy Spirit abiding in us. We are not called to be "spectator Christians" but to be "overcomers" who will conquer the ways of the world, the flesh and the devil—especially when these ways infiltrate the teaching and practice of the Church. Jesus gave us His call and His promise in Revelation 3:21-22: " 'He who conquers I will grant him to sit with me on my throne, as I myself conquered and sat down with my Father on his throne. He who has an ear, let him hear what the Spirit says to the churches.' " "He who conquers" (or "overcomes") refers not to fighting each other—but rather to overcoming the forces of evil that are sometimes subtly (and very often flagrantly) trying to take over the Church, the nation and the world! We today have the same challenge to withstand evil. "And they have conquered Him by the blood of the Lamb, and by the word of their testimony, for they loved not their lives even unto death" (Rev. 12:11).

A pastor writes: "For me, VMTC Prayer Counseling has been a freeing, a strengthening and an undergirding experience. I had been shaped by the emotional absence of my father, culminating in his suicide when I was nineteen, and the sweet controls of my mother, which made it difficult for me to know what I really wanted! I became a Presbyterian minister, interestingly enough initially to please her, but later to serve God. Like many mainline denominational people, I was deeply influenced during my college years by the humanistic philosophy I majored in and the Greek-based psychology I studied in my graduate work; and through books and movies. I even worked as a counselor in a psychiatric clinic where I know that I was able to help people, but mostly through human help and knowledge.

"It was (and is) such a joy to be *freed* through VMTC Prayer Counseling: to know that I can confess as sin, repent of and ask God's forgiveness for all of the humanistic and secular thinking and reading and acts of my life! What a joy to discard from my library some books which had always made me feel very nervous anyway. I still have most of my theological and psychological books and the secular, psychological knowledge—but, as Anne White says, it is the *long* way to help people who will not accept the Scriptural conditions of VMTC Prayer Counseling! What a joy to be freed from the need to try to control everything, to try to be president of every group! What a joy to be freed to face conflict, not fearing that conflict would destroy me or those around me—because now I know that I *know* that God is in charge!

"It was (and is) such a joy to be *strengthened* through VMTC Prayer Counseling so that I am not frightened by thoughts from the past, or made helpless by the 'wounds of the past' such as those inflicted unknowingly by my parents, or by people's words. I know that I can immediately claim God's help and power! It is such a joy to be *undergirded* through the Scriptural teachings and practices of Prayer Counseling. Each morning I put on my spiritual armor like Christian in Bunyan's PILGRIM'S PROGRESS and know that God is with me to help me each moment of the day and night. It means so much to me to be able to pray for help and wisdom immediately. I will fail now *only* when I insist on having my own way as His available power is greater than any need that I have. Praise God: Father, Son and Holy Spirit!" Now, that he himself is free, this pastor can *really* preach the Good News to set others free! What a joy to be free—to be genuine!

World evangelization is a response to Jesus' Divine Commission given to us when He said: "Go therefore and make disciples of all nations" (Matt. 28:19). But, *we need to evangelize the Church*, also! Most pew-sitting members are not even aware of the power of Jesus' Victory or even of the reality of Satan as their personal adversary. Nor do they realize when they decide to follow Jesus seriously (with *real* personal commitment) that they will have the same personal enemy (the adversary) who used even one of Jesus' disciples to betray Him in the attempt to destroy Him! Satan fell from heaven because of rebellion against God and he is still creating rebellion in the Church—whenever and wherever the Church *seeks to bring in the Kingdom of God on earth* as it is already established in Heaven. When people are living lifestyles of rebellion against God, Satan can use them as his tools by influencing them with demonic thoughts—especially when they open the door of their minds to his false teachings of pagan, "demon-worshiping" religions. Witchcraft today is on the increase and it uses psychic powers, dabbling in mind-control and out-of-body astral traveling as well as magic and spiritualism—all of which are forbidden to those who truly believe in and follow Jesus Christ as their personal Savior and Lord! Jesus did *not* teach us to be "broad-minded" or liberal condoners of these false teachings and practices that are part of an "occult explosion" which seeks to become accepted even by the Church in some areas today! In fact, Jesus said: "Enter by the narrow gate; for the gate is wide and the way is easy, that leads to destruction, and those who enter by it are many. For the gate is narrow and the way is hard, that leads to life and those who find it are few" (Matt. 7:13-14). And again, He warned His disciples saying: "I am the way, the truth and the life; no one comes to the Father, but by me" (John 14:6). So, if any of you think that I am too narrow-minded in this, perhaps you need to talk to Jesus about it because *He* is the one who made this clear to me!

Thousands of people (too many to count) in each of many countries have been set free from this demonic oppression through VMTC Prayer Counseling—praise God! Jesus said that He came to set captives free and give sight to the blind. Spiritual sight is even more important than physical sight! The "drug explosion" and the "sex explosion" are linked in with the "occult explosion"—as is very evident to all of us who counsel in depth the many distressed people who have lost their spiritual sight and wandered into the enemy's territory. Unfortunately, Satan plays for keeps— Jesus forgives and heals us! When we recognize and repent of our sins and ask His pardon, He can and will heal and restore us!

If you, dear reader, are one who is playing "Russian Roulette" with your life, thinking that you can get away with habitual, prolonged sins, you need to *stop now* and ask Jesus to forgive you! Tell Him that you are truly repentant— not just sorry for yourself or that you've gotten caught—and ask His pardon for every sin you are now naming *specifically* —as well as for all those sins that you do not now recall. Ask Jesus to forgive you for your sins against your own body— but also for your sins of reaction against others. Ask Him to forgive you for every sinful, wicked, lustful, hateful, angry thought (or word) that you can ever recall—no matter how long ago or what the circumstances happen to have been. Do *not* rationalize—REPENT! Promise Jesus that you are now *with His help* going to *turn away from this mess* you've made of your life! Acknowledge that you cannot possibly do this—or live from now on—without *His* help. Ask Jesus to come into your sinful heart now and clean out all this confessed garbage of the past. His Blood was shed for you personally and He can redeem your past life and give you His

The Drama of Redemption

Peace in place of the burden of guilt that you have been carrying for so long. *Ask Him to be LORD now*: to take charge of your life, to be your Master in place of the other gods that have been controlling your life. Begin to thank Him for His forgiveness whether you feel like it or not—standing on the promises in I John 1:9: "If we confess our sins, he is faithful and just, and will forgive our sins and cleanse us from all unrighteousness." Trust in the authority of God's Word—not your previous, preconceived ideas. Believe that you *have* received and you *will* receive.

Praise Him now as an act of your will—regardless of your feelings! You may have had a dramatic release through tears followed by an upsurge of His Joy—or you may not. You have asked—now, believe that Jesus is trustworthy and will be true to the promises of Scripture. Accept the fact that He has not only forgiven you but is also cleansing you with His perfect, pure Blood. Thank Him that *His Holy Spirit now lives in your heart* and accept His Peace! You have now been re-born in the Spirit! If you have honestly meant all of this, you are now a child of God and an inheritor of the Kingdom of Heaven. This means much more than that you will go to Heaven when you die: it means also that you now have the Holy Spirit abiding in you to lead you into the Truth that glorifies Jesus so that you can experience His Joy and Love and Peace in your life *from now on as you follow Jesus* who is your Lord and Savior! He is also your Healer and Redeemer—praise God!

Some years ago, two VMTC Prayer Counselors ministered to a woman (whom I'll call Martha) who was furious at her father because he had sexually abused her as a teenager and had committed incest with her sister who had a child by him as a result. For years Martha had hated her father—but she had tried to repress this anger. A few days before this Prayer Counseling appointment, she had learned that her father had recently forced himself sexually on his fourteen year old grandchild and now the girl was pregnant! Martha was so enraged that she wanted to kill him—but friends persuaded her to be Prayer Counseled first instead of going to the jail to tell her father how much she hated him and wished he were dead! It took the grace of God and seven hours of VMTC Prayer Counseling for her to be set free from the spirits of anger and murder that had taken control of her. She argued and stormed that she would never forgive her father—but in the end, she was able to see her own sins of thought, the anger and murder in the spirit, that she needed to confess to God. Lovingly and patiently, her two Counselors showed her that in order to experience fully God's forgiveness, she would have to forgive her father for all that he had said and done to her sister and to his grandchild as well as to herself (Mark 11:25). By the mercies of God, Martha was able to do this—at first as an act of her will—and then to her amazement, the Heavenly Father's Love enabled her to *feel the reality* of that forgiveness for her earthly father. She could at last forgive the sinner even though, of course, she did not condone his sins! When the session finally ended, she had received the empowering of the Holy Spirit to hold this Victory, this new freedom to love and forgive! Although it was getting late, Martha knew that she had to go to the jail to see her father and tell him about Jesus and His forgiving Love. When she tearfully told her father that she forgave him for every one of his sins, he looked at her and then burst into tears. Martha led him to the Lord—and a new Peace came into his heart. They talked about his new life in Jesus and she embraced him with real love as she said good-bye—for the first and last time, as that night he went home to the Lord!!

THREE

FROM A "WALKING WOUNDED" TO A "WALKING MIRACLE"

*T*he "healing of the whole person" involves total healing which is far more important than physical or mental or emotional healing alone. It involves the healing of relationships because none of us is an island! It took a relationship with two human beings for us to be born—as well as a relationship with our Heavenly Father who from before the foundation of the world called our lives into being. For any of us to become whole, there must be a relationship with Jesus Christ for it is only in Him that "our release is secured and our sins are forgiven through the shedding of his blood" (Eph. 1:7 NEB). When we accept Jesus Christ as Lord and Savior (as we have seen in Chapter 2) a new relationship is formed with the Holy Spirit: we are "reborn," born of the Spirit. Scripture reminds us that no one can call Jesus Lord except by the Holy Spirit (I Cor. 12:3b).

Many years ago, as I ministered to people in Prayer Groups and at Healing Services of the Church, the Lord showed me that most people are the victims of their own sins or of the sins of others—or often a combination of both! It was also clear that those people were usually unaware of the "Spiritual Warfare" going on in their lives. All too often they were blaming God when, in fact, the root cause of their problems was the work of the enemy who had tempted them to sin and to turn away from the healing that only Jesus can bring to distressed minds, wounded spirits, disturbed emotions, sick bodies and broken relationships! As I looked about me, the Churches seemed to be filled with "walking wounded" instead of "walking miracles" — as in the early Christian Church.

Confession of sin opens the door to God's healing forgiveness which, in removing burdens of guilt, often has led to healing of spirit, soul and body. This has for centuries been a part of the ministry of Roman Catholic and Episcopal (Anglican) Churches. And in John's Gospel, we read that Jesus said to the crippled man at the pool of Bethesda (after He had healed him): "See, you are well! Sin no more, that nothing worse befall you" (5:14). Although sins of the spirit and of the mind and body are obviously not always the cause of *dis*-ease, medicine has taught us through the study of endocrinology that our emotions release glandular secretions which can cause serious illness; and that the thoughts we hold in our subconscious minds have a profound effect on the autonomic nervous system, i.e., the functioning of our bodies. Many doctors tell us that emotions such as fear can make us more subject to catch diseases, more accident prone, more vulnerable to heart trouble and high blood pressure, for example, as well as allergies and even some forms of cancer. In Psalms 32:3-4 we read: "When I declared not my sin, my body wasted away through my groaning all day long. For day and night thy hand was heavy upon me; my strength was dried up as by the heat of summer." The Psalmist acknowledged his sin, no longer hiding his iniquity but confessing his transgressions — and then the Lord forgave "the guilt of (his) sin" (vs. 5). In Proverbs 17:22 we read: "A cheerful heart is a good medicine, but a downcast spirit dries up the bones."

From a "Walking Wounded" to a "Walking Miracle"

The soul includes the will, the emotions, the intellect and the subconscious mind—whereas the spirit is that part of us which, when yielded to the Holy Spirit, can give us true direction in our lives. When we live in the soulishness of our emotions or our intellects, we will not be "aglow with the spirit." A spirit of fear which entered early in life may be quenching the Holy Spirit in us so that instead of being able to overcome fear, we are, in fact, being overcome by fear! For example, we may will to live in the power of the Spirit and yet in fact be so overcome by some past experience of fear that it dominates our responses today. Instead of acting on the basis of the present, we may be reacting because of some controlling, buried emotion or painful experience (often without knowing specifically why this is so).

The more I ministered to people, the more I realized that they were often the victims of the sins of others—even before they reached an accountable age and sometimes in the womb stage of their lives. Thus, it was not their sin but a case of being sinned against that caused the *dis*-ease (whether mental, emotional or physical). Obviously, the matter of healing of relationships became even more important! After many years of praying for the Lord to show me a better way to help people, He revealed to me, step by step, an effective pattern of Scriptural, balanced, life-changing prayer that depends on the counselee accepting the authority of God's Word, the shed Blood of Calvary and the loving ministry of two (or three) trained counselors who listen and pray through to victory—using the gifts of the Holy Spirit. Now, over 20 years later, this Prayer Counseling is taught under the safeguarding authority of Victorious Ministry Through Christ, Inc. in Clergy Schools (including Australia, Canada, Finland, Sweden and Pakistan). The VMTC Prayer Counseling team consists of a man and a woman (whether clergy or lay) who are called by God to this Spirit-led but disciplined ministry. After they have been trained in 3 or 4 intensive Schools with practical experience as well as balanced Scriptural teaching, the gifts of the Holy Spirit operate most effectively within the confines of the Word of God—undiluted by man-made techniques and solutions. This method of VMTC Prayer Counseling has been translated along with my basic book, HEALING ADVENTURE, into several different languages as the need is universal for this Scriptural, careful, balanced, in-depth healing ministry. Total commitment to Jesus is the only price paid by the counselee.

In one case a pastor's wife, a fine, committed Spirit-filled young woman was becoming totally neurotic with fear that even kept her from going to the basement to do the laundry! Over a period of several years, various evangelists and church members (as well as her own gifted, loving husband) had ministered to her but to no avail. Her increasing terror had no medical solution and her husband was at his wit's end because of her very real suffering and the repercussions on their two young children—and even the Church. Well-meaning people telling her "to name it and claim her healing" only made matters worse! She was totally unable to help herself—and yet various sessions of regular deliverance ministry had left her worse off than before! Finally, she and her husband traveled over a thousand miles to one of VMTC's Schools—and there the Lord's healing Power transformed her from a "walking wounded" to a "walking miracle"—praise God! She has since become a very effective Prayer Counselor and has been used by the Lord to extend His healing Power to others.

In that same school, in the last session of Prayer Counseling, her husband (as an intercessor) was used by the Lord to bring the "word of knowledge" that released the Director's 16 year old son from crippling headaches which were preventing David from being able to keep pace with his High School class. His doctor had arranged for every possible medical test (including CAT-Scans) but no cause could be determined for these intense headaches that were progressively getting worse and had seriously affected David's scholastic record. Even when he wanted to be well for special sports or family outings, these headaches would suddenly come upon him for no apparent reason. The hidden cause (as identified by the Holy Spirit in that night's Prayer Counseling session) was a particularly horror-filled TV program that David had watched as a 7 year old boy one night: his parents were at Church and the babysitter had broken their rules! As the "word of knowledge" was given in the form of a question, David re-lived in anguish the violence of those horrendous scenes of terror that had been so deeply repressed in his subconscious mind! The Love of Jesus cast out all the repressed fear that had affected his automatic nervous system by causing those repeated, violent headaches—and David was *joyously freed to live*! The Power of the Holy Spirit overcame the power of evil to set this young captive free— and now he is in college, living a full life.

This excerpt from a Church bulletin is based on Philippians 4:8-9: "A TV set is only a machine—glass, metal, wires, and little gadgets—until you place it in your house. . . . In some houses, TV becomes a baby-sitter, for babies of all ages. In other houses, TV is a narcotic, an escape from reality. Or it may be a thief, stealing time, thoughts, friendships, creativity, and opportunities for much-needed reading, recreation and family companionship. In too few houses, TV is a servant, providing worthwhile entertainment. What TV becomes *depends on you*, the user! If you accept it as a tool, use it sparingly, wisely, and purposefully, it can become a servant. If you accept it as a friend, *watch and listen continuously*, it will become your master!"

Some years later, both David's father and the young pastor whose wife was healed have become members (along with ten other pastors) of the Board of Directors of Victorious Ministry Through Christ under whose authority I am privileged to serve the Lord as Founder and President. At least two members of our very active Board of Directors (along with five or six other well-trained pastors and several senior women counselors) staff with me each of VMTC's Clergy Schools of Prayer Counseling. Members of our committed, ecumenical Board of Directors have also worked abroad with me to transplant this Scriptural and effective Ministry in other countries. Each Board Member has for himself (or herself) experienced the blessings of this Spirit-filled Ministry which God has entrusted us "to give to the Church." He has not only personally been blessed in being himself set free to live in new effectiveness, but has also found this to be a valuable, Scriptural tool in his Church's ministry. The healing of the denominations (as well as the healing in relationships with other countries) evidences in an important way the measure of the Spirit of God at work through VMTC Ministry—so that the wounded can be healed and the Lord Jesus can be glorified as He uses us to set captives free, give sight to the blind and open prison doors (Luke 4:18-19)!

This witness by a Presbyterian Pastor's wife speaks for itself:

"I was a product of my parents' conflicting desires. My mother conceived me despite her unwillingness and was duty bound to care for a child that she could not love emotionally. My father's part of this conflict destroyed both their oneness and bound him to the child of his insistence in a protectiveness and affection that was both smothering and idolatrous.

"The affection of my father was dependent upon my actions and a single mis-step produced a separateness and loneliness that filled me with doubts about my worth and his words of love. Fearing that I would cross the limits of his love, I lived carefully and endeavored to be as pleasing as possible. Mother took excellent care of me physically, but only once was I in my mother's arms. It was Christmas and I was allowed to sit on her lap. I feigned sleep in order to hold on to that brief moment knowing all too soon I would

From a "Walking Wounded" to a "Walking Miracle"

fail her and say in true sorrow, 'I'm sorry, Moma.' Her reply was as certain as my apology, 'If you were really sorry, you wouldn't have done it!' It was the litany of my childhood. Something was wrong in our family and most assuredly it was me! From this rejection, even before my birth, I became fearful of life and relationships. Like Job, those things I feared kept recurring and I grew into adulthood desiring security that no relationship provided. I feared people would get to know the *real* me and find out how absolutely worthless I was.

"I perceived the Heavenly Father in the limited and distorted relationship I shared with my parents. In spite of years of Bible study, a Christian college and my earnest desire to please God, He became the one who loved those He chose and loved me not at all or only because it was His duty. He seemed to be fickle and not to be depended upon — because I was not worthy of His Love.

"The one thing I could grasp was that my husband was given to me as a parable of the Father's love. He was the only person I ever completely trusted and in all of our years together he had never rejected me — not once — not in the good times and never in the difficult. Daily, he told me how beautiful I was and that I was more precious to him than any save the Lord. God placed me in his committed care and often reminded me that my husband's love was a parable for what greater truth I needed. He was preparing me for the deep healing that no one person could give me . . . the healing of the whole of me . . . the removal of crutches and of festered wounds!

"My day of release came in 1983 when my husband and I entered a VMTC Clergy School of Prayer Counseling to learn how to help others (not realizing how desperately my husband and I needed help). No band-aids were plastered on the old wounds, for in that time of spiritual surgery the Holy Spirit did a thorough cleansing and healing of all the pain of a life time! For the first time, I knew that the Father loved me and declared me His own beloved child. He wasn't angry with me! I belonged! Fear fell away when rejection and worthlessness were cast out of me and the words 'accepted in the beloved' came alive and have lived in me each day since. Today I walk tall and straight and life in His Love is an adventure! My loyalty to VMTC Prayer Counseling is deep and abiding as I can now abide in Jesus: the old torment is gone and I'm really alive! Praise God!" The writer and her husband are now released VMTC Prayer Counselors — using this ministry to the Lord's Glory in their Church!

God's call to us Christians is a call to holiness without which there can be no true wholeness. Paul's prayer is meaningful to us today: ". . . and may the Lord make you increase and abound in love to one another and to all men, as we do to you, so that He may establish your hearts unblamable in holiness before our God and Father, at the coming of our Lord Jesus with all his saints" (I Thes. 3:12-13).

FOUR

GOD IS FAITHFUL

*I*n today's world where faithfulness is often a missing quantity, we need to build our house of life on the faithfulness of our Lord as revealed in His Word. It is He who calls us to Total Commitment and He promises to give us His Grace not only to make that surrender of our wills to His—but also the Power to fulfill the commitment we make! He does not leave us comfortless or helpless in the quicksands of today's world. He is the God of Peace who Himself will sanctify us wholly, as Paul wrote so convincingly to the Thessalonians in one of the closing paragraphs of his first Epistle. Paul prayed that your "spirit and soul and body be kept sound and blameless at the coming of our Lord Jesus Christ" (I Thes. 5:23). This is the *wholeness* we Christians need—not just healing of the body but also healing of our spirits, our wills, our emotions, even our intellects and especially our subconscious minds. Since our relationships affect all of these, we obviously need the healing of our relationship with God the Father, God the Son and God the Holy Spirit. We need the healing of our relationships with others so that we can love (and forgive them) regardless of their attitudes to us. In the command that Jesus gave to the questioning lawyer, we can see a somewhat hidden relationship: "to love your neighbor as yourself" really implies loving yourself—because hating yourself has an adverse effect on the way and extent that you love your neighbor (Matt. 22:37-38)!

A father who was secretly cheating on his wife became hyper-critical of her and their children until finally he had made the whole family so miserable that counseling was necessary. When he confessed to God his sin of adultery and was forgiven, the burden of guilt fell off him and he could love his fine family. He no longer had to tear them down with criticism and could praise God for His Peace. God promises in His Word to be faithful: to do *His* part! But what about *our* part? Because He gave you and me freedom of will, we can choose whether or not we will be faithful to Him. We can be rebellious and reject His Will for our lives. *Or*, we can be double-minded—blowing hot and then cold—saying one thing and doing another. *Or*, we can put idols on the throne of our lives so that they usurp our Lord's rightful place! Even though we may call Him Lord, we may in fact be saying: "Lord, move over—as someone else is more important than you are in my life." *Or*, we can try to escape from God's Will through drugs or cigarettes or alcohol dependencies, and also through too much busy-ness that crowds Him out of our priorities. *Or*, we can let apathy divert us from fulfilling God's intentional purposes for our lives—always putting off till tomorrow what we know needs to be done today. *Or*, we can escape through fantasizing as we live in a dream world based on soap operas, movies and TV shows rather than in the real world where we are called to live and carry out Jesus' commission to help bring in the Kingdom of God! We can be our own worst enemies!

Sarah was a woman who was addicted to soap operas and was neglecting her home-making as well as being cold to her husband because his love-making did not measure up to her idols in her imaginary world. As part of her commitment to God in her VMTC Prayer Counseling session, she gave up that and other addictions. The Lord showed Sarah how He could use her gift for meal preparation to plan a week-day "Fellowship Lunch" for the people who came to the noontime Thursday Communion Service at their Church —before they returned to work. The lunch was tasty and priced so reasonably that soon husbands began to meet their wives for worship followed by the delicious fellowship meal. Other women joined her in this successful service project— not to make money but to help bring couples to their Church's weekday worship services. Sarah's time and gifts became a new outreach ministry for her Church. She found joy in the reality of her new way of life!

God has called all of us to be His sons and daughters in Christ Jesus! This is not something we can do on our own. The success story painted by the humanists (including "charismatic humanists") is not the Victory that overcomes the world—because we cannot overcome in Jesus' Name and Power when we are tainted by the world! If our values and priorities are as materialistic and self-seeking as those of the world, we Christians will not be that people set apart to bear fruit as Jesus abides in us. If we are only concerned about what we can *get from God*, we are not really following the Master who *gave up His very life* to save the world from its sin! When you and I replace "Jesus-centeredness" with "man-centeredness" we are following not the Cross but the temptation of Satan to try to sit on God's throne. The devil's way (as we have seen) is one of ambition, pride, violence—and this led to his fall we are told in Scripture (Is. 14:12-15 and Ezek. 28:14-17). The closer we come to Jesus, the more eager Satan is to break up our loving relationship with Him (as well as with others). By manipulating people and circumstances, Satan tries to oppress us. As in the case of Job and many of us who have had to resist the devil in today's "Spiritual Warfare," Satan tries to harass us in the hope that we will succumb to his oppression and "curse God and die" (Job 2:9). As mentioned earlier, the enemy tries to deceive us into hopelessness so that we will give up and deny God's Power to bring His Kingdom into our hearts and lives. This is especially the case when we are serving Jesus in a ministry that sets Satan's captives free.

But *God is faithful!* He who calls us to Himself is not going to desert us! Though we may grow weary and impatient and cry out "How long, Lord?", we are not forsaken. The answer may come in unexpected ways—even ways we would not have chosen. But God promises in His Word to make a way where there is no way of escape—so that you and I can endure it (I Cor. 10:13)! The way of escape may be to love that difficult person or to forgive him or her. It may be to go on persistently praying through to ultimate Victory—even when the enemy (and some of our friends) tell us that the situation is hopeless! It may be to go on living in a crisis that seems interminable; or to carry on a ministry and forgive others who back away even though they themselves have been blessed. It may be that the way of escape is to go on rejoicing in the Lord's strength when our bodies are strained and our energies drained by the selfishness of those whom we had expected to stand with us. It may be that the way of escape can come only through our own broken-ness even though the immediate cause is the sin of someone else for whom we pray!

"God is faithful, and He will not let you be tempted beyond your strength, but with the temptation will also provide the way of escape, that you may be able to endure it" (I Cor. 10:13b). This has recently become one of my favorite Scriptures as I have had to live it out in the "laboratory of life." Praise God! His Word does not fail us! We can trust *in* Him!

In the fall of 1986, it was confirmed to me that the time had come to sell my house and move our VMTC Central Office from my home where it had been located for over 17 years. For a very long time, my name had been on a waiting list for a house in a lovely Christian retirement community which would provide total maintenance and maximum security—features that would make it easier for me to travel in the Lord's work when the office was no longer in my home.

One day the phone rang and I learned that my name was now at the top of the list and suddenly a house was available — it was mine to accept or reject almost *immediately*! I had just put my house of 20 years occupancy on the market — but the real estate agents were dismayed by the fact that heavy traffic on the street immediately in back of me was discouraging their prospective buyers. When the city widened that street, they put up huge signs declaring 25 mile speed limits — but they so rarely ever enforced these limits that the street had become a noisy interstate connector! I had to keep forgiving the city for this negligence which worked a hardship on me when already the Winter Park area was a "Buyer's Market" with 12,000 houses for sale! This injustice was especially maddening as I paid very high city taxes!

At the time of the street widening 15 years before, the Lord had clearly guided me to landscape (mostly with my own hands) our ½ acre of land with exotic, luxuriant shrubs, vines and trees to offset this disadvantage. At that time as Dick was convalescing from his second heart attack, I had prayed for the guidance and strength to create a lovely, landscaped view from each window. The Lord had guided me to combine plants so that something different was in bloom each month of the year — in order to bring the outdoors into each window's view for my husband to enjoy. Last winter, I thanked God each day and rejoiced at the glory of the profusion of azaleas and camellias that blossomed under the spreading arms of our huge, old oak trees. They were more beautiful than I'd ever seen them! Each time that a freeze was threatened I prayed for my heavily laden orange tree to be protected — remembering also those who had large groves with their livelihoods at stake. Each day by nine o'clock my house had to be ready for inspection — but I watched again and again the loss of interest by prospective buyers when they walked into the office with four desks, a typewriter, a computer with two printers and a storage closet full of books! Although the noise of the heavy traffic was not noticeable inside the house and everyone commented on the excellent condition of my home with its well-built, thick walls, it was obvious that it was going to take a miracle to sell as *quickly* as was necessary a 35-year old house under such adverse conditions!

The Lord guided me after intensive prayer to take the leap of faith and buy the *new* house—which involved taking out a mortgage—so that at the end of the year I was financially committed to two mortgages plus two insurance premiums, two tax bills and two heavy maintenance expenses! Each step presented overwhelming problems but the Lord over-ruled as I threw myself continually on His Grace for His guidance and strength. Just before Christmas, He had led me to put my house on a "Sale by Owner" basis and there was an exciting flurry of interest while I could be at home to show the house. But, in four weeks, I had to resume my schedule of speaking engagements—so it was necessary to list with another broker. While I was in California, the Lord gave me the clear words "Your house has been sold"—so I came home fully expecting that a couple who had been seriously interested were at last able to buy my house! To my chagrin, the agents said that the deal to sell their town house in another city had fallen through! This was shattering—because Satan was nagging at me that I'd lost the Lord's guidance. However, that same day a couple to whom I had shown the house at Christmas time, came to see it again—bringing their relatives. We intensified our prayers on that crucial weekend. While in prayer with a longtime prayer partner and friend, the Lord clearly guided me to telephone this couple and offer to reduce the price which evidently brought my house into the range of another one they had been almost ready to buy! A few days before, I had been advised by my son and also by one of VMTC's Board members that I would lose appreciably by not reducing the price under these unusually unfavorable selling conditions. The Holy Spirit confirmed to me the wisdom of their needed advice.

God's faithfulness had also provided tangible guidance through another friend who called me just before Christmas to say that his corporation was sending VMTC a check for $5,000.00 to pay for the year's rental of an office in a commercial location! This was truly a miracle—the largest single gift that VMTC had ever received! That telephone call was my best material Christmas present—for it released me from the burden of feeling that I needed to sell my house at a price high enough to provide office space for this Ministry. With the prayers of my family and friends as well as our VMTC Family, my Rector and the Bible Study/Prayer Group of our Church—and with the much needed help of my stalwart associate and my Christian attorney—the contract was signed at last! I had to forgive the buyers as they had cut my already reduced price and delayed for six interminable weeks the process of getting their loan while they held endless inspections of my house. God was faithful in carrying me through this real "war of nerves"! It was almost ridiculous how Satan attempted to delay and defeat this whole process at *every* turn! My prayer partners and I prayed daily—sometimes several times a day—over each disappointing delay, each major decision and each crucial challenge. As we were literally in "hand-to-hand combat" with the enemy, we were constantly wielding the Sword of the Spirit (the Word of God) and holding up the Shield of Faith!

In the midst of all this, it was increasingly obvious that Satan was trying to break me down under the pressure of these harassing, delaying circumstances in hopes that I would cancel Schools, Missions and a Retreat that the Lord had assured us were *very* important to Him! It was frustrating to carry out this house sale and complicated move while I was flying to and from California or Georgia or Maine or New Jersey or driving to South Florida for these strenuous speaking engagements! Traveling deadlines barely meshed with moving deadlines, and office work was barely completed in preparation for these VMTC commitments—as well as for our Annual Board of Directors' Meeting in April! At these times, it was comforting to know that Paul had struggled against Satan's opposition to his plans: "because we wanted to come to you—I, Paul, again and again—but Satan hindered us" (I Thes. 2:18).

The Lord was faithful! In each crisis, *He carried me through* the most horrendous move of the twenty-one I've made, including those to Japan and England many years ago! Never before have I felt that I moved while going to and from the airport! Helpfully, my associate moved the office to our new location on the weekend that I moved most of my belongings to the new house. He was barely home from a trip to Wyoming on the day that the movers arrived early to take my heavy furniture to the new address—although weeks before that I had moved out many household items, most of my clothes, the rugs and the lighter pieces! Again, the Lord was faithful in giving Don the wisdom and physical strength to help me in this strenuous job—as well as providing miraculously good weather. Daily, I shared the burdens in prayer with faithful intercessors—especially when Satan used inefficient workmen and senseless delays to make the move of my home and office even more confusing and difficult. Daily and hourly, I had to depend on "I can do all things in him who strengthens me" (Phil. 4:13). Daily and hourly, I had to keep submitting myself and the many frustrating complications to God, forgiving others and resisting the devil. I knew that if I did this, my persistent enemy *would eventually have to flee* (James 4:7)! Even those who were helping me in the move were under attack in this "Spiritual Warfare"—and yet each round was won as we continued in prayer to claim the Lord's Victory and press on by faith, despite physically and emotionally exhausting circumstances! *God is faithful* to overcome what Satan intends for evil with good— *but,* He expects us to "wield the weapons that are divinely powerful," *to persevere in His Power* when our hearts and bodies would otherwise fail under the pressure of the evil one who opposes and harasses us! Satan's strategy is to try to keep us from fulfilling God's purposes for our lives. Jesus has already won the Victory—but *we have to live it daily* by His Grace! I confirm what Paul wrote in his Second Letter to the Thessalonians: "Finally, brethren, pray for us, that the word of the Lord may speed on and triumph, as it did among you, and that we may be delivered from wicked and evil men; for not all have faith. But the Lord is faithful; he will strengthen you and guard you from evil" (3:1-3).

Now, as we work in our new and larger office and I rejoice in the beauty and peace, the security and comfort of my convenient new home, I continue to praise God for His faithfulness. My heart rejoices over the many, unexpected blessings He has provided for me in this new Chapter in my life. I have had no desire to cling to the old home although it was a joy for twenty years. No wonder Satan tried *so* persistently to rob me of this Victory! Where God guides, He provides—in this case more beautifully and abundantly than I had ever expected! He says clearly, *daily*: "FOLLOW ME!"

During one of the heaviest days of "Scriptural Warfare," the Lord gave me this prophecy: "You have cleared the decks for action for fuller service to Me and I will use you in a new way, my daughter, my beloved daughter. I will give you a new ministry through a new book and I will open new doors for you and your life will become more effective for Me."

FIVE

TRUST IN THE LORD

*B*elief is more than intellectual assent. We can believe that Jesus is divine, the Son of God, but this is not the same as believing *in* Him, putting our *trust in Him*, staking our lives on His Reality — as the early Christian martyrs so obviously did when they went to their deaths singing hymns of joy! To believe that Jesus performed many miracles during His earthly, visible ministry — and even that He still does miracles today through His Body the Church — is not the same as believing *in* Jesus' Love and Power to heal us at this moment of need! How often people ask: "Why is it harder for me to have faith for myself than to pray for others?" When you and I have the pain, it takes a deeper sense of trust in the Lord to replace that insistent ache or fear or discomfiture. How, then, will we "grow this trust in Jesus" so that we will not be faint-hearted when the crises come in our lives? How can we hold fast and trust in Jesus when Satan attacks us? When doubts assail us? When the doctors give us no hope?

Perhaps, *one way is to saturate ourselves with the Word of God.* As we read each Scripture, God reveals Himself to us through His Word "which will not return to Him empty or void" (Is. 55:11). There is the "logos" word — and often as we are reading the Bible, the Lord gives us His "rhema" word: a confirmation in our hearts that this is *His specific word for us* in some particular situation. We need to check our guidance as we test this word to be sure that it is of the Lord because the enemy can also quote Scripture (as he did to Jesus in the temptation to throw Himself down from the pinnacle of the temple). Sometimes, the "rhema" word lies dormant before we are called upon to use it. Sometimes, it becomes a steady refrain in our hearts. Sometimes, we need to "live it out in the laboratory of life" before we see its real significance to us — acting out our faith. In actual fact, we need not only to stand firmly but also by faith *to begin to act upon the Word*: "Take delight in the Lord and he will give you the desires of your heart" (Ps. 37:4). We need to be sure that the desires of our hearts are suitable to be accepted by God! It is not really "rightly dividing the Word of God" if we use this Scripture (and other similar faith promises) to try to force God to do for us other than *His* Will! In many teachings today the word "presumption" is more accurate than the word "faith" because Scriptures are lined up purposing to make God do what *we* want Him to do—when, on the contrary, we should align ourselves with *His* Will as in Jesus' clear teachings and the witness of His Life. Jesus said that He came to do the Will of His Father—and He went through Calvary!

Some claim that "Faith Formula" teaching makes human suffering unnecessary and that they have a new, superior "Higher Revelation" so that they are not on this subject bound by what the Word of God says! This is a dangerous form of "charismatic humanism" because they claim in promoting the "Prosperity Gospel" the same fancy clothes, fine cars and extravagant houses that the humanists claim! Isn't it odd that Jesus was so out of touch with this "Higher Revelation" that He had to ride into Jerusalem on a borrowed donkey! Isn't it odd that there are so many New Testament Scriptures that warn true believers of sufferings that they would need to endure? Apparently, Paul and Peter did not have this "Revelation Knowledge" either—nor did Dietrich

Bonhoeffer who wrote in THE COST OF DISCIPLESHIP: "When Christ calls a man, he bids him come and die" (p. 7). Of course, obviously Stephen as the first martyr was really out of touch with the "Higher Revelation" which claims that suffering is no longer necessary! According to this aberrational teaching, such Scriptures as Romans 8:16-17 and II Timothy 3:12-13 are ridiculously out of date for charismatics of the "Faith Formula Gospel" today! The promise Paul makes is that: "When we cry, 'Abba! Father!' it is the Spirit himself bearing witness with our spirit that we are children of God, and if children, then heirs, heirs of God and fellow heirs with Christ, *provided we suffer with him* in order that we may also be glorified with him" (italics mine). In writing to Timothy, Paul said bluntly: "Indeed, all who desire to live a godly life in Christ Jesus will be persecuted, while evil men and impostors will go on from bad to worse, deceivers and deceived" (II Tim. 3:13).

"Now faith is the assurance of things hoped for, the conviction of things not seen" (Heb. 11:1). A more modern definition might be "Faith is living within the conditions of the answered prayer." Faith in Jesus involves trust in Him who is *totally trustworthy*! When people reject us or let us down in life, it may be helpful to remember that Jesus is the *only* One we can totally trust because He is God Incarnate. As one six year old explained to a little friend: "Jesus is God come to visit us." In Psalm 37:5-6 we read: "Commit your way to the Lord, trust in him, and he will act. He will bring forth your vindication as the light and your right as the noonday." Too often we try to bring forth our own selfish vindication and usually make the problem worse—instead of trusting the solution to the Lord. We usually have to learn this kind of trust by being obedient to Him in many little situations—so that when the crises come in life, we will be able to draw on that faith as a person draws a check confidently on his bank account when he has a financial need—providing he has been putting money in that bank! It is the "daily-ness" of commitment—even moment by moment *trust in Him*—that God wants of His children. So often we try to run ahead of Him and solve our problems instead of waiting patiently on Him. *Jesus is the Answer*—and He will make a way where there is no way—but our fretting and anxieties only hold back His solution to the situations.

The Psalms warn us not to put our trust in wealth (44:6 and 46:6-7) or in leaders (146:3) but rather in God's Name (33:21) and in His Word (119:42). We are also told by Jeremiah not to trust in man (17:5) or in works (48:7). Paul reminds us in many places as well as in Ephesians that we are not to trust in our own righteousness (3:13). We are encouraged in many of the Psalms to accept the goodness and loving, kindness of God (31:19; 32:10, for example). There are benefits promised us such as deliverance (22:4-5); blessedness (4:4); and provision (37:3-5). In times of "trial by fire," it is most helpful for those in danger or persecution to read Psalm 56:1-4; or Proverbs 3:5-6, when we are in need of guidance. Our God is faithful—but we need to saturate ourselves in these and other Scriptures which help us to counteract the lies that Satan uses to cause discouragement or doubt in hopes of lowering our level of faith!

We need to learn through continual practice to know the Voice of the Master—just as sheep learn to know and trust the voice of their shepherd. In today's world with its many conflicting, clamoring, insistent voices, it is especially important for us to learn to know the Voice of our Good Shepherd and not be taken in by the wiles and deceits of the devil. Jesus will not contradict His Word—so it cannot be the guidance of the Holy Spirit if a seeming solution is contrary to the "rightly divided Word of God." There needs to be (as a basis) three Scriptures confirming each other—not just one isolated Scripture. The "whole counsel of God" needs to be taken into account when one is seeking guidance—not just some single circumstance that we'd like to think of as a confirmation of our plans. The "gift of discerning of spirits" is a very much needed one today; and we should learn to use the other two revelation gifts of "wisdom" and "knowledge" in conjunction with the "gift of faith" when we seek guidance from the Lord. Too many people fail to "pray things through" — instead they jump to an unwise conclusion too quickly and then "repent at leisure." If God has called us to do something, we need to continue to trust Him to bring about the fulfillment of His purpose in the situation under question — but we need to be willing to be part of the answer also (if He so chooses).

Too often we have a desire for a "quick fix" in today's world. Everyone seems to want "instant everything" — but God does not always work on our time-tables. Sometimes He seems exasperatingly slow when we are weak in our trust. As we grow the fruit of patience, we come to realize that He is "right on time"! A pastor's wife (on reading this manuscript) shared with me a prophecy that was fulfilled nine years later when they were called to pastor their present Church. God prophetically revealed to her: "I have a people called by my Name. These you shall lead into green pastures of worship and *I* shall cause the growth." Her beautiful music ministry today is a fulfillment of this prophecy.

Usually, *in seeking guidance we need to get a "rhema" word from the Lord — and confirm that with a wise counsellor before we take "the leap of faith."* We certainly need to check whether the course we have in mind is Scriptural and whether it is really in the Name (Nature) of Jesus — not just in line with our own usually selfish natures. If our proposed plan of action is self-exalting, vindictive or motivated by "escapism" it is not of the Lord even though some circumstances point in that direction. "Tough love" is being loving even when it is difficult — and it usually means wanting the highest good for the other person. When in doubt, it may be best not to do or say or write anything — until the Lord clarifies His Will. There will come a time when the lights turn green and we will need to proceed cautiously in faith — continually praying for the Lord's confirmation through His Peace in our hearts as we move ahead, trusting in His Wisdom and Strength to carry us through to Victory. Sometimes He moves swiftly—at the very last minute!

Doubt and unbelief are often Satan's tools to try to rob us of our effort to "trust in the Lord—and in the strength of His might" (Eph. 6:10). In Psalm 37:7, we read David's advice: "Be still before the Lord, and wait patiently for him; fret not yourself over him who prospers in his way, over the man who carries out evil devices!" It is difficult for us to be patient—especially when evil is prospering and that does not seem to us to be just. Our envy is often clothed in self-righteousness when we see "wrongdoers" prosper. We forget that although they may have material benefits, they will not have the *real* prosperity of "heart peace with God"! Yet, we will be the losers if we let envy or anger or fretfulness break a hole in the hedge of protection about us. Satan will take advantage of these reactions to circumstances to make us lose this inner peace that God has promised us when we are centered in His Will. "Thou dost keep him in perfect peace, whose mind is stayed on thee, because he trusts in thee. Trust in the Lord forever, for the Lord God is an everlasting rock" (Is. 26:3-4). What a wonderful spiritual legacy we have in these words! This Rock will not move away from us—although sometimes we move away from Him! When our minds stray away from *His* Will, we need to return to Him with repentant hearts. We can trust His Word that God will always forgive our confessed sins and remember them no more (Heb. 8:12)! One modern translation says: "roll and repose [each care of] your load on Him . . . and He will bring it to pass" (Ps. 37:5). We often fail to "roll" the problems over to the Lord—more often, most of us do not really "repose" them there for we take them back too soon and begin to try solving them ourselves!

When I left Orlando Airport for Karachi, there was no need for a Pakistan visa on my passport—a point I had checked out earlier that week. After a refreshing overnight in Frankfurt, Germany I had dragged my bags up to the

Pan Am desk to check them in on the noon flight to Karachi — only to be told that I could not board that plane because I had no passport visa and the Pakistani government had at midnight just dropped the ban! No amount of reasoning would persuade the ticket agent. As I prayed for divine wisdom, I recalled that my late husband had always told me: "When in trouble, ask to speak to the top man" — so I did, the Lord Himself! However I was also guided to ask to speak to the Pan Am Supervisor in Frankfurt. When he finally came to the desk, I heard myself asking him: "What would you do if I were your relative?" Somewhat taken aback, he finally agreed to call the Pakistani Consulate in Bonn, Germany. After much discussion he informed me that I needed to travel two hours by train to that capital city to get the necessary passport visa. The plane I wanted to board was leaving in a half hour!

I had been praying in the Spirit all this time and realized that I felt rooted to that spot as I had no German money, no contacts or place to stay in Bonn, and the next plane to Karachi would leave three days later! I would miss the Retreat I was supposed to lead! Obviously, I would not be able to rendezvous as planned with our VMTC Director who had left New York at 9:00 P.M. the night before and was on the plane anxiously waiting for me to board this suddenly "verboten" flight! Quietly within me I heard the still, small voice of God: "Go in faith, nothing doubting." It was *so* faint that I said: "Lord, please turn up the volume! I have to know at this instant what I'm to do and only You can make this decision for me!" Again, I heard the exact same words — a little clearer, but nothing more! Suddenly I heard myself saying to the Supervisor: "I'll take the chance of being deported on the next flight from Karachi if the Pakistani Government will not let me stay for 14 days without a passport visa — but please let me board this plane and join my colleague as I can't go to Bonn. If I did, it would be too late for my engagement." He telephoned and finally agreed to take my luggage on that flight—providing I took "full personal responsibility"! This meant that if I were deported from Karachi, I would waste my U.S. $2,300.00 plane ticket and would miss my important speaking engagement! By this time, I had asked the Lord to give me a third confirmation and the same words came very clearly: "Go in faith, nothing doubting!"

On the plane at last, I was overjoyed to pray with our VMTC Board member, Fr. Al, about this crucial decision. Then the Holy Spirit through him confirmed my guidance as he said: "I think it's going to be all right when we get to Karachi. The Lord is going to work a miracle!" We praised the Lord and on the very long flight, we worked over the many detailed plans for the VMTC Retreat and School which he was to co-lead with me. We felt the Lord's leading that I was to give him the elaborate Scheduling Sheets and the Teaching Outlines—just in case! (I have learned from long years of experience in constant "Spiritual Warfare" that when Satan finds he cannot upset things, he usually calls off the attack!)

As we left the plane in Karachi and proceeded to the Passport Control Desk, an American businessman in line ahead of us was overjoyed to find that Al lived very near him in New Jersey. When the Pakistani agent asked for his passport visa, the excited businessman burbled something senseless which confused the situation. The Lord used this distraction in an amazing way. One of the Passport Desk personnel, in the confusion, suddenly reached out, grabbed my passport, stamped it "14 days" (in spite of the fact that I did not have the required visa) and waved me through to safety—praise the Lord! I could have been locked up in the airport detention jail and deported on the next flight to Frankfurt three days later—thus forfeiting my expensive ticket and missing altogether the purpose of my trip! TRUST IN THE LORD! His ways are *wonderful* to work miracles in our lives! Trust and rejoice!

SIX

PRAISE CHANGES US

*P*raise comes naturally to us when we are really "walking in the Spirit of the Lord" because our spirits were created to enable us to respond to the Holy Spirit. The Scriptures tell us that God inhabits the praises of Israel (Ps. 22:3). So if we want to be in Christ, we will discover that praise is necessary to this fulfillment we seek. "Enter into his gates with thanksgiving and into his courts with praise"! (Ps. 100:4). Thanksgiving may be the avenue we need to travel as it leads us through the outer gates to the inner courts of praise. We thank God for what He has done for us and for what He *is doing* for us *now* — and, *in advance*, for what He *will do* in the future as we continue to trust in Him. But we praise God for *who He is* — regardless of whether or not He is answering our prayers the way we want Him to do! "Praise" and "Adoration" are always the highest forms of prayer.

A friend was at first tempted to blame God when her daughter's fine plantation home burned to the foundation one morning some years ago. It destroyed all their furnishings and clothing! But then she realized how thankful she needed to be because their lives were spared! Had the fire occurred at night, they would have been drugged by the smoke as they were sleeping upstairs. She began to praise

God for His Mercy. It was wonderful how their friends rallied to their need and showed their love in many tangible ways. The Lord has blessed them with an even more beautiful house — He not only saved their lives but restored their home!

When we yield ourselves to praise our Heavenly Father, we are joining with the whole company of heaven! No wonder it has been said that "praise changes things" — but perhaps it can be even better said that *praise changes us*! When we praise God during the difficult days, we are making "a sacrifice of praise to God, that is, the fruit of lips that acknowledge his name" (Heb. 13:15). This admonition in Scripture uses the word "*continually*" — so obviously there will be times *when we do not always feel like praising God*. As an act of will we can make this an offering of obedience to Him for who He is — regardless of our feelings.

A friend was praying for her mother who was seriously ill. It was so easy to worry as the doctor's diagnosis was alarming for one of her age. My friend prayed to know *how to pray* and the Lord gave her the inner conviction that she was to relinquish her mother to Him and then just continue to praise Him! Within a few days, much to the doctor's amazement, her mother was totally healed! We need to do this as a way of bearing fruit, acknowledging His Name in the midst of the crisis, the pain and the grief of the circumstances of our lives.

When my mother was in her early nineties, she suffered a broken hip from a serious fall. The doctor told us that she could not survive the excruciating pain unless she had a hip operation — but he warned that the operation might not be successful. Mama assured him that she was a Christian and was not afraid to die — but she added that she did *not* want to linger on if she could not get well! Unfortunately, she never really recovered from that operation and was being literally kept alive with a catheter, I-V feeding and other artificial life-support measures. To my grief, she was not mentally right after the operation! She was what she had said that she did not want to be: a "vegetable" propped up in a wheel chair. My talk with her doctor was frustrating: he could offer nothing more for the future! I knew that my mother, who had been a dynamic person, would recoil from being in such a degrading, helpless, useless state! She had lost her faith some years before when she wandered into Christian Science and other cultish teachings. But, praise God, she had returned to her faith in Jesus through the ministry of her young Episcopal priest who anointed her with oil for healing of her sight! (see HEALING ADVENTURE, Anne S. White, Logos, p. 66; Sovereign World, Ltd., p. 61) After that, living in an excellent nursing home, she had been a faithful intercessor for the other patients and was loved by all the nurses. I knew from our prayers and previous, long conversations that she was ready to meet her Master — but medical science was forcing on her a degrading, dependent existence. In despair, I went with a close friend to the Wednesday morning Communion Service at our Church — hardly knowing how to pray except that if the Lord wanted her to come Home, He would have to take her! When I knelt at the altar rail, I forgave the doctor and repented of my anger toward him. I felt that he had gone back on his promises to her. Then I relinquished my mother to the Lord and began to praise Him for His answer to my prayers. On arriving at the nursing home an hour later, the head nurse met me to say that my mother had just a few minutes before breathed her last breath. She was safe in the Nearer Presence of Jesus — already joining with the whole company of heaven, praising God at His Throne of Grace! As my husband said to the nurses: "After a long and fruitful life, she has at last gone Home to the Lord!" Her funeral service was a joyous "Graduation Service." Alleluia! "The strife is o'er, the battle done, The Victory of life is won . . . Alleluia!"

When we are in an attitude of praise during "Spiritual Warfare," the Lord's Resurrection Power works more effectively in us and through us. Often in our Central Office, when one of our VMTC Schools of Prayer Counseling is having serious difficulty because registrations are slow, a couple (who really need to come) will call to cancel their reservations. The Lord usually guides us to pray with them on the telephone and claim together the Victory of Calvary over the situation—such as illness, or baby sitter problems, or finances. When we hang up the phone, we continue to praise God that the situation is in *His* hands and thank Him in advance for the Victory! In one case, the wife called unexpectedly to cancel their application and was unconvincing when I asked why. It was clear to me that this couple *really* belonged in the School—and that they were unaware that this was "Spiritual Warfare." I prayed with her on the phone against a spirit of confusion and asked her to pray with her husband that night. Our office continued to praise God for His guidance—and the next morning she called excitedly to say that the confusion had cleared away and they were coming to the School! In other cases, we have prayed with couples by taking authority over the spirit of infirmity which was attacking their sick child. We continued to praise God; and the very next day, the husband called to report that the child was well again—praise the Lord!

It is not always easy for us to praise God during difficult stretches in our lives. At those times, we have "to make a sacrifice of praise"—as an act of our wills, regardless of our feelings! Satan is the deceiver of the elect—and, as we have elected to follow Jesus, he will tell us that the situation is hopeless. The enemy's chief weapons are deceit, doubt, discouragement and depression when he is trying to keep us from praising God. Those are the times it helps us to use our "prayer language"—to pray in the Spirit. Praying in tongues seems to help "energize" the other gifts of the Spirit so that we can better hear the word of wisdom or knowledge that God wants to give us in that situation. Those who downgrade the gift of tongues do not realize its usefulness—for when we do not know how to pray, the Spirit prays through us with groanings and utterances that we do not understand (Rom. 8:26).

As the author of Hebrews says that we are *continually* to praise God, the reference may be to this gift because we can pray in our prayer language continually while using our intellect to drive our car, for example. Otherwise, it would be difficult to pray in the intellect "*continually*"! The Letter to the Hebrews tells us that the continual "sacrifice of praise to God . . . is the fruit of lips that acknowledge His name" (13:15). Joy is one of the beautiful fruit of the Spirit.

Satan has also been called "the accuser of the brethren" and he frequently uses this method to distract us from praising God. His technique is first to deceive us through attractive temptations so that we will fall into his trap of sinful thoughts or words or deeds. Once we have sinned, Satan accuses us and tells us that we are hopeless and helpless — and that God will never forgive us. Satan will even mis-quote Scripture to do this. He uses a pincer method on us: one side is deceit and the other side consists of nagging condemnation. We need daily to recognize the enemy's tactics and protect ourselves from them. One way is to begin each day with a fresh, joyous commitment to the Lord as we seek in His Word the message that He has for us that day. We need to spend time praising Him — not dumping our petitions on Him as we enter His Presence! When we begin each day in an attitude of praise, we can in faith expect His miracles throughout the day and we will be better prepared for Satan's unexpected attacks. We also need the protection of the whole armor of God — especially the breastplate of righteousness. (See Ephesians 6:13-17 and Chapter II in TRIAL BY FIRE by Anne S. White.)

If we succumb to our enemy's false accusations, it will quench the spirit of praise in us. When we fall under condemnation about something, it may be wise for us to ask the Holy Spirit to convict us if there is a hidden sin involved. Sometimes, that "still, small voice of God" shows us a resentment or a fear or some pride in our hearts — something that needs to be confessed as sin. If so, we need to repent and ask

God for His forgiveness, claiming this blessing instantly as we stand on the promise of I John 1:9. The Word tells us here and in many other places that God forgives our sins as soon as we repent and confess them to Him. After that, the enemy has no legal right to accuse us. If God remembers them no more (as we are told in Hebrews 8:12) then who are we to carry guilt any longer? We can tell the accuser to leave us as we stand on the promise of Romans 8:1: "There is therefore now no condemnation for those who are in Christ Jesus." We need immediately to turn to praising God for His loving mercy: He removes those sins as far as the east is from the west! (Ps. 103:12). Praise God! As Christians, we can always praise God for making salvation a reality in our lives through the Victory at Calvary of His Son Jesus. And, through the empowering of His Holy Spirit, you and I can change our life styles from fear and self-pity, from bitterness and defeatism to praise *Him* all through the day! Hallelujah!

Praise is so vital to us in our Christian walk today. It implies faith so that we praise God in the midst of our difficulties; and this, in itself, helps us to crucify the flesh nature that might want us to wallow in self-pity. Praising God when circumstances are going awry helps to clear our channels *to receive His guidance* for the solution to the problems. Praising God quenches idolatry when we humans are apt to exalt the man (or the ministry). Most certainly, when we are praising God, it supplies strength to follow His guidance whatever and wherever the need.

At one of the Karachi Clergy Schools of Prayer Counseling, we had unusually heavy attacks by the enemy because our other International Team Members (coming from Australia and Finland) were also affected by not only the sudden passport visa problem but also by the hijacking of the Pan Am plane at the Karachi Airport about midnight as it had just flown in from India! As mentioned in the last chapter, by God's miracle, Fr. Al and I had arrived from our harried flight about midnight on Monday. We were leading a Thursday to Saturday Weekend Retreat with the Bishop and his local Team. As there was no telephone communication anywhere that week, we did not even know of the terrible catastrophe until two days afterwards when his wife brought out to the Retreat Center the two Australians who had arrived safely and had left the Airport just a few minutes before the cruel hijacking disaster began! Paivi was still ashen-faced as she told us the tragic story—and suddenly the Lord showed me that had He not rescued me miraculously, I would have been involved! I would either have been boarding that hijacked plane (if the Pakistanis had put me in jail and deported me); or, had I gone to Bonn, Germany to get a visa (as the Airlines wanted me to do) I would have been in the bloody shooting at the Karachi Airport as I was disembarking from the Pan Am flight from Frankfurt. That plane always crosses in Karachi with the West-bound flight from India—the one that was so brutally hijacked! I began to praise the Lord for His merciful guidance and protection—and I spent my free time that afternoon in my room praying for the many injured and the families of all those who were killed. I was so thankful to my God who protected me!

In that School, we simply had to keep on *"praising the Lord, anyhow"* because the oppression of the enemy in that Moslem country was *so* great! Dysentery hit us all at different times, but as we kept praising the Lord, He healed each of us just in time for our next assignment! The Finns and Australians had to make unforseen, inconvenient visits to Pakistani passport authorities because they also had to arrive without visas. We kept on praising the Lord because there was really nothing else we could do as *everything* was *so* confused under this heavy Satanic attack! Amid shouts of joy, they arrived back at the Center at the exact moment they were needed to start the 5-hour Prayer Counseling appointments—which, had they not been able to do, our School's whole closely meshed schedule would have been disastrously disarrayed! Praise not only changed these situations but *it certainly changed us*!

Inadequate food, vicious mosquitoes, sultry heat, brushing our teeth in a cup of boiled water, cold showers, no telephone contact when we badly needed it—none of these adverse conditions daunted our praise of God who had brought all of us through our travels safely. He empowered us to lead the most effective Retreat and School that we have ever had in the Christian "Monastery of the Angels" in the center of a Moslem city during the time of the Islamic religious festival when deafening broadcasts (night and day) claimed allegiance to Allah! As we prayed in the Spirit almost constantly—the last thing at night and the first thing in the morning as well as throughout those eleven pressured days—we praised our God, the true God revealed to us in Jesus Christ, the Creator and Sustainer who is worthy to be praised! Hallelujah!

SEVEN

TERMITES IN THE HOUSE OF LIFE

*I*n many parts of the world, termites are a dreaded danger because, like a hidden, silent army, they attack the wooden structure of a house and even its furniture. The outward appearance may not reveal the damage that is being done secretly. When an infestation of termites is discovered, a house must be sealed by professional exterminators in an enormous plastic covering so that the poison applied can penetrate thoroughly every piece of wood to destroy these wood-eating insects and their larvae. Periodic checks must be made thereafter to be sure there is no recurrence. It is most unlikely that anyone would ever buy a house unless it had been thoroughly inspected and guaranteed to be termite-free.

What about the "termites" that breed in the house of life? Often, like those that eat away and destroy wood, we find "spiritual termites" that eat away at relationships to destroy them. The fears that often creep into a child's heart can be hidden there—unidentified—until years later the problem becomes exposed because it is damaging to a relationship. For example, a friend as a tiny girl, leaned over on a pier to reach for a little basket on the bottom of the ocean and, losing her balance, she frantically splashed into the water! As she came up gasping for breath, people laughed at her—but no one rushed to rescue her! By then, fear of drowning gripped her heart. When finally she was hauled out of the water, what others considered funny had become a nightmare for her! Because it is natural for a person to repress unpleasant events, she had totally forgotten this incident. However, fifty years later when her husband decided to take up sailing as his special hobby, she was panicked! Her fear of water intensified as she faced the thought of having to trust herself to the hazards of sailing. Even her love for her husband and her desire to share his new hobby could not overcome the gripping fear of water whenever she stepped aboard his prize possession, that glistening white sailboat! It seemed silly for a competent, mature Christian woman to be so terrified—and her husband was beginning to get impatient with her excuses, her reluctance to join him in his favorite past-time. Worst of all, he would soon retire so that sailing would be a daily problem! When she came to me for Prayer Counseling, we asked the Lord to show her the hidden cause of her fears—to set her free from the bondage to this unknown root. In the Love of Jesus, she unexpectedly re-lived the incident that had been so terrifying! She experienced His healing of the devastating fear that had secretly been holding her in bondage. She was totally set free by the perfect Love of Jesus that casts out fear. Her husband is delighted that she can now "crew for him" as they take exciting trips on their boat. Praise God!

Perhaps even more serious are the fears of disease that often stem from illnesses of a parent (or of another child) during the early years of life. "To fear cancer is the best way to get it," a Christian doctor remarked to me once as we were discussing the physical effect of buried emotions such as fear, resentments and self-pity. Fear of poverty can often warp the life of those who grew up in a home during the depression—so that they cannot enjoy spending in a normal way even though money is not a real problem for them today. There is an unnatural and unwarranted bondage to money. Fear of sexual molestation is a horrible curse on the life of a child who is forced to live in a home where a stepfather (or an uncle) threatens harm if the dreadful secret is revealed. Fear of rejection because of some early failure to please a harshly exacting parent can become more crippling as other rejections "latch" on to it later in life, thus contributing to further painful relationships.

All of these fears are "spiritual termites," hidden devourers, that eat away at relationships secretly causing *dis*-ease; and often they are aggravated over the years by the very fact that the original causes have become buried in the subconscious minds of the ones who have repressed them— or even deliberately suppressed them! "Out of sight, out of mind" is a slogan that does not happen to be true. Thoughts held in the subconscious mind have a powerful effect on the autonomic nervous system. A person who has had a "death-wish" for many years can become "accident-prone" or develop some rare disease. There are other fears that, although buried for many years, can still be affecting a person's relationships today: fear of confrontation, fear of height, fear of the dark and fear of death. Fears generated by some violent horror story seen by a child on TV (or in a movie) can cause serious spiritual, mental and physical repercussions years later. All of these can be healed by the powerful Love of Jesus who can heal the yesterdays of the past because He is "the same yesterday, today and forever" (Heb. 13:8).

Resentments are an equally serious breed of "spiritual termites." Often the person cannot recall the cause of the problem that has been harbored for years: a secret poison that eats away at his heart. A young man who suffered from sporadic attacks of nausea and headaches came to me for VMTC Prayer Counseling because the attacks were becoming more frequent—thus seriously hampering his work as well as his family life. The Lord gave me a "word of knowledge" that the cause was anger against his mother. He was astounded because he had not been aware of this repressed emotion. The Holy Spirit revealed the beginning of these symptoms: at the time when he was a boy of 13, his mother had to leave him alone in the hospital because of the critical illness of another child. Although intellectually he had accepted this need for her to be away from him, the experience at the time had caused severe feelings of rejection and anger. Because it was not acceptable to show anger, it had been deeply repressed—until the Holy Spirit brought the whole experience to light and healed him as we prayed in thanksgiving for Jesus' release of his body, mind and spirit from this crippling past relationship. Of course, he had to forgive his mother! The Holy Spirit can reveal the buried past in order to heal it.

Self-pity is often characterized by a grumbling or murmuring habit. The Israelites were guilty of this sin after God had delivered them from bondage in Egypt. They complained about the manna and the quail instead of praising God for His deliverance of them from their former cruel task-masters. They wandered in the wilderness for 40 years until that generation died off before they could enter the Promised Land. Are we grousing about our every day circumstances instead of praising God? Do we let the problems outweigh the blessings in our lives? The more we wallow in self-pity, the greater the problems will become—until we see our need to praise God *in* all situations or circumstances! Also, self-pity doubles the load we carry and keeps us from seeing how God can intervene and overcome with good what Satan intends for evil.

Rejection is another "greedy termite" in the house of life. If we are sure that we are going to be rejected by someone, we can become very sensitive in a self-centered way, suspicious of all that the person does. Carrying a chip on our shoulders only encourages someone to knock it off!

Those who carry rejection from early childhood accumulate more and more rejections as they grow up. It may be that they heard directly (or overheard indirectly) that they were not wanted — that it was economically a burden for the parents or that they wanted a boy instead of a girl. Secretly (and often unconsciously) such a person will set herself up to fail — so that she can accumulate more rejection. As this process continues in the formative years, the child (now grown up) continues to expect and fear rejection. Similarly, it is hard to be the wife of such a person as all too often the husband (who has developed a life-style of rejection) will not accept love from those who love him the most! To accept love would destroy the pattern of self-pity with which he is most comfortable.

One serious rejection in childhood can begin a damaging habit of accepting rejection where it was not intended. Each fresh rejection brings more loneliness until the Love of Jesus can be brought to bear on this person's life. Many people are not in touch with past areas in their experiences because they have been made to feel like a "non-person"; and, having repressed so many painful emotions, they become "loners" and feel a depressive attitude even when things are going well for them. The buried cause may be a father who punished his son too harshly — or for something he really did not do. Or, it may have been a mother who nagged continually, never showing praise, love and approval when the child had done his best — his utmost — to please! To succeed in sports or school and yet not receive needed approval from parents is a rejection that may lie dormant for years until the confused person "grows up" within the loving acceptance of two trained Prayer Counselors who are letting the perfect Love of Jesus flow through them as an antidote to years of repressed rejection, inadequacy and fear of failure. These "spiritual termites" breed others such as rebellion, anger, even confusion of identity.

When a child is brought up in a truly Christian home, such feelings should be discussed and prayed for at the time they occur. The love and acceptance of wise, Christian parents can help insulate the child from wounds of the spirit inflicted by others. In such instances, to learn how to forgive is a most valuable lesson that Christian parents can teach their children.

Blaming others can become a destructive habit in a child who grows up where discipline is too harsh. He has to resort to this "escape mechanism"—and sometimes to lying—because he cannot face the pain of admitting defeat. Such a habit of continually making excuses (if accepted by the parents) leads to failure to take responsibility for one's own actions in later life. This breed of termite ultimately makes the person more careless and forgetful because he has learned that he can get away with shifting the blame—instead of facing up to failure and learning to overcome it in his daily relationships.

The termite of rebellion can be seen in the following:

"As a child growing up in a pastor's family, I was the last of four siblings. Even before I entered school, my father was a working pastor. He preached to a small congregation on Sunday, and worked at a gas station the rest of the week. That left very little time to spend with me. My oldest brother, who is eleven years older than I, had the responsibility to watch over me. He became a father image to me. I must have idolized him, because when he got married at the age of nineteen, it really hurt me that he was leaving our household. I began looking to my peers for acceptance. I thought that there was a need to prove to others I was normal. All through high school I tried to drink and smoke more than anyone else. I would go to dances, which was against my father's will. To build up the nerve to ask a girl to dance, I would get drunk. Being drunk caused girls to be repulsed by me, so I drank more to escape the rejection. Before I graduated from high school, I moved out of my father's house because I was too rebellious to live by his set of rules.

"While attending junior college I met the lady who would one day become my wife. A year and a half later, I was drafted into the army. I told her that I didn't want to be engaged to her because I didn't want her to feel obligated to me if I came back only part of a man. My experience in Viet Nam was terrifying to say the least. I was a foot soldier which means you carry everything on your back while splashing and stumbling over hill and through jungle in search of the enemy. You never knew but that you would be killed next! Whenever we got back to a firebase, we would try to escape from reality by doing drugs. The mood was one of fatalism so I simply lived for the now and whatever pleasure through which I could escape from life.

"After spending my time in Viet Nam, I came home looking pretty much the same on the outside. However, I was a powder keg on the inside. Very soon after coming home, we were married. My new wife learned how different I was. I would vacilate from a weeping, insecure, childish person to an angry, over-bearing tyrant. I abused her verbally and even physically at times. Nine months after we were married, we both recommitted our lives to Jesus. That made things better for a while. However, I still felt a rage inside whenever someone made comments like, 'The real heroes are those who ran away to Canada.' I was angry at those who drafted me, those who sent me to Viet Nam, the officers in command, the Vietnamese that didn't accept us G.I.s, and all the people back home that didn't care or were even skeptical about it all! I watched the news as 'The Last Marine' left the U.S. Embassy. I could not help but ask myself, 'Why did I risk my life over there?' Any chance I got, I poured out my wrath on anyone near, especially my wife and family.

"After five years of marriage, I noticed the beginnings of a physical problem. I was retaining liquids which caused my legs to swell. My condition continued to get worse; and finally, after almost a whole year I went to see a doctor. He immediately put me into the hospital. I was told that my kidneys were failing and was put on medication and a special diet. The doctor said that at best, we could hold it in check. There was also the possibility that I would need a kidney transplant! During the two weeks that I was in the hospital, I had a visit from a friend. He told me that the Lord wanted to heal me inside, as well as healing me physically. That next December I attended my first VMTC Clergy School of Prayer Counseling. I didn't think that I needed any help, but I wanted to learn how to help others. The next month after going to that school, I had the last appointment with my kidney specialist! I'm no longer on medication and I'm certainly not on any diet.

"Things *began* to improve, but I still had a problem with being rebellious to any authority. I had been working at the Post Office almost ten years when, because of my rebellion and unsubmissiveness, I managed to get fired. For six weeks I had no job to go to each day, and that gave me plenty of time to talk to God. Because I had learned the importance of confession of sins through VMTC Prayer Counseling, I knew what to pray about. I'm convinced that because of my confession and God's forgiveness, He not only gave me back my job, but He added another blessing. I now have a special job, training manager, and I have learned how to communicate and problem-solve by working together with those under me. God has allowed me to work with problem employees, just as I used to be, to help them learn to cooperate and work together. I now get the privilege of praying for people in offices for miles around as I meet with them on a weekly basis.

"There is no doubt in my mind, that God had to heal me *first* before He could use me in this way. Praise the Lord, for HIS mercy endures forever!"

The Lord can and does "cleanse with His Blood" when the person is willing to let the penetrating Light of the Holy Spirit reveal these root causes. The Love of Jesus heals but usually the person has to see the sin of letting these "spiritual termites" take over in his or her life. Often the one so affected by the sins of others during childhood years has, in condemning them, sown the seed to do the same thing to his (or her) children. Jesus can exterminate these "spiritual termites" as the Power of His Holy Spirit replaces in the house of life the power that Satan has had because of buried, repressed, damaging emotions. But, obviously, the person so affected has to be willing to look honestly at these areas of need and confess his (or her) own sins as well as to accept the Love of Jesus to heal the areas where they have been the victims of the sins of others. What Jesus did at Calvary is truly effective for the healing of those who will accept Him—not just as Savior and Healer but as Lord and Master! A new life style of "walking in the Spirit" is not only desirable, it is necessary to maintain the Victory won over these "spiritual termites" in the house of life!

EIGHT

FORGIVENESS IS A BEAUTY TREATMENT

*T*he old Adam lives in the unbeliever who has not accepted Jesus Christ as his Lord and Savior. Unless we die to self and accept the reality of Jesus' power to save us from our sins, Christians can be in the Church and not be aware that their commitment is to an institution but not to Jesus who is its Head. Paul, in writing to the Roman Church, said: "You also must consider yourselves dead to sin and alive to God in Christ Jesus" (6:11). Our salvation is *in Jesus* — not in some particular ritual or counselor or popular preacher. Jesus is the One who brings us into that right relationship with God, our Father, so that we come alive in Him — out of the deadness of our past fears or bitterness, our pride or rebellion, our rejection or grief, our lusts or other abuses of our bodies. When we repent of these sins with a broken and contrite heart, God forgives our sins and the Blood of Jesus our Savior cleanses us from all unrighteousness (I John 1:9). The adversary tries to accuse us, to tell us that we are not forgiven but God's Word says that He removes our sins as far as the east is from the west (Ps. 103:12) and that God "remembers our sins no more" (Heb. 8:12). If God forgives us when we repent and confess our sins (which Scripture assures us that he does), who are we not to forgive ourselves? We are then guilty of the sin of pride if we say: "God may forgive me but I cannot forgive myself." We then need to confess that sin of pride, also!

One man of 70 had been a member of his Church ever since he was a small boy. As a teen-ager, he committed a sin that for many years he had felt was unforgivable. He continued to go to Church but he seemed to have no peace in his heart. He was hard to get along with—critical of others so that he had few friends. He seldom smiled and seemed to find little joy in life. When I was speaking in that Church, he came to a Saturday morning workshop. I had been watching his face as he insisted on sitting alone on the back row and seemed not to be really listening. As I was explaining God's forgiveness, this older man suddenly began to listen with an interest I had not previously noticed in him. Unexpectedly, he called out, "Sister, do you mean that God would forgive a sin no matter how long ago it was committed?" I replied confidently quoting the two above-mentioned Scriptures. Suddenly his face broke into a broad smile as he shouted "Hallelujah"—and immediately he looked 20 years younger! The burden of his guilt had truly rolled away! Praise God!

How many people carry heavy burdens of guilt that warp their relationship with God, with others and with themselves. When we feel guilty, we try all too often to ease the burden by pointing the finger at someone else. If we can feel that we are better than someone else, we can rationalize away our guilt—or so we often think. After all, the psychiatrists usually explain away guilt (unless they are practicing Christians) by saying, "Well, everyone else is doing it." The humanists say, "If it feels good, do it." No amount of rationalization or self-justification or "blame shifting on someone else" will take the place of truly penitent confession of sin. God created us and He knows best our sins. If we have difficulty in quieting our consciences, it is usually wise to make that painful confession to God in the presence of a pastor or trained lay counselor who will be able to claim God's Word with authority—whether it is called "absolution" or "assurance of pardon" (James 5:15-16). It is not only Scriptural but helpful to have a witness so that if later on Satan tries to accuse, he can be told that he is a "liar and a thief"—trying to rob the forgiven sinner of one of the benefits of Calvary! How true is the song "He paid a debt, He did not owe, I owed a debt I could not pay." Yes, you and I can only receive that grace of forgiveness with thankful hearts because Jesus paid the price with His Life's Blood. No wonder that the humanists reject the Biblical story of creation—so that they won't have to confess their sins to the God and Father who created them! After all, if we only evolved from a protozoa, we would not have to look to God for our moral code. Ethics can become situational with no Ultimate Judge. No wonder our country is beset with increased crime—even among the best educated and intellectual citizens. The gods of intellect and education have been worshiped too long—and now we are seeing (through scandals in sports, on Wall Street, in business and in government) that these gods have feet of clay.

If one is confessing sins to God in the presence of another human being it is very important to know that this other person will keep strict confidentiality. Gossips are not recommended for this kind of ministry. It is most certainly true that one can go into one's closet to confess sins to God and be forgiven; but the Scripture in James 5:16 stresses: "Confess your sins one to another so that you may *be healed*" (italics mine). There is an amazing blessing that comes to one who has carried an unbearable burden of guilt when he (or she) hears a fellow believer express whole-heartedly our heavenly Father's forgiveness in a *personalized way*! Usually, this guilt has been buried for many years —repressed because the thought of the sin was too painful. The truth is that all of us have sinned and fallen short of the glory of

God. The forgiven sinner can now "worship the Lord in the beauty of holiness" (I Chron. 16:29 KJV). Yes, the thought of worshiping and praising God in the beauty of holiness is also repeated in the Psalms. As the Heavenly Father releases His forgiveness, the new joy becomes a beauty treatment—spiritually but also physically!

Sometimes this blessing has come to an older woman who long years ago had an abortion and never dared to tell anyone about it. Most often the penitent is one who committed fornication and has found that the guilt as a result of that sin has later seriously interfered with the marriage bed relationship where guilt in connection with sex has marred the joy of a God-given union with their marriage partner. In an amazing number of cases, children who have been sexually tampered with (usually by relatives or family friends) carry a tremendous burden of secret guilt—even though they are the ones who were sinned against. They are usually made to lie about this or are threatened to fear that exposure will bring severe punishment—so the secret may have been kept for 40 years or more. One person went into hysterics because the release was so great that she could not control her feelings—but for most people there is a tremendous response of joy! Of course, there is also the need for that person who has been abused to verbalize his (or her) forgiveness of the one who caused it. Incest is increasing—or else victims are being more open about disclosing such harmful family situations in their relationships. Wounds from such experiences are so deep that only the Love of Jesus can heal them.

Although the world (and sadly enough some sectors of the Church today) claim that homosexuals cannot be healed, this is not true of Christians who are willing to ask for and receive their healing *on God's terms*. Sin must be confessed—and there are ample Scriptural references to the fact that homosexual relationships are sin. Factually, homosexuality is sin because it usually destroys the possibility of a meaningful, holy marriage. The independent spirit in the homosexual causes him to seek sexual gratification for selfish reasons with no responsibility for a child that might result. The same is true of the lesbian person. Since such persons can be set free by Christ, it is a parody for the Church (of which He is the Head) to condone the ordination of homosexuals or lesbians in direct disobedience to pointedly clear injunctions of Scripture (Rom. 1:26-27; I Cor. 6:9). Again, humanism is slipping into the Church to distort the Word of God. "Christian Humanism" is a mis-nomer because all humanism is an effort to replace God's Power with man-centeredness. The lure of many of the cults is "to become God"—which obviously is a lie of Satan's fabrication. Most likely the persons who succumb to that lie do not even recognize that there is a devil who is deceiving them into their supposed "glory trip."

The same "god of this world" deceives gullible people into thinking that reincarnation is true—which, thank God, it is not! We are clearly told (in Hebrews 9:27 as well as in other Scriptures) that there is *no* coming back. What a hoax is being perpetrated on greedy people today who are investing money so that when they return in their next incarnation they will have quadrupled their investment! Such rubbish sadly gets the attention of people who are weak in their faith and ready to grasp at the next exciting way to make a fortune! There is no way that a Christian can believe in the false teaching of reincarnation because Jesus is both the "expiation" and the "propitiation" for our sins: that is, He has not only paid the debt but He has also satisfied the need for the debt to be repaid. As all pagan religions teach reincarnation, it is not only sad but also dangerous for Christians to read about them: to "give heed to deceitful spirits and doctrines of demons" (as Paul warns us in I Timothy 4:1). In Chapter 4:3-4 of his 2nd Letter to Timothy, Paul describes well what is happening today: "For the time is coming when people will not endure sound teaching, but having itching ears they will accumulate for themselves teachers to suit their own likings, and will turn away from listening to the truth and wander into myths."

In a far away country, I had the joy of ministering in VMTC Prayer Counseling with a Lutheran Bishop to a Pentecostal pastor who came to our Clergy School of Prayer Counseling to be trained to minister to others in this effective way of Spirit-filled prayer. John, at that time, gave me permission to use his life-changing story. When he was a young lad in his teens, John had run away from home and was rebelling by searching for "truth" in every false, pagan religion and in every occult practice he could find—without ever realizing that he was really hungering for a true relationship with God! A bad relationship early in life with his earthly father had blinded John from finding the true God. And these spiritual sins (as well as many others) separated him from the Love of God! After John was set free from these bondages to the past, overwhelming joy filled his heart! He kept repeating: "I found Jesus when I was saved, and I found the Holy Spirit when I was baptized in the Spirit—but now, through this ministry, I have at last found my Heavenly Father! I am in my forties—but now I know that in Jesus, I am God's beloved son!" John (not his real name) has eagerly gone on with VMTC Training. He has been graduated as an experienced counselor (with his lovely wife) to be God's conduit to set captives *free to live* in the Power of the Holy Spirit because of Jesus' effective Victory at Calvary and in the wonderful Love of their Heavenly Father and Creator! John received a "beauty of holiness" he had never before experienced. In gratitude to his loving Heavenly Father, he has already been used to minister joyously this new freedom to others who also have been blind (as he was) in that they were seeking Truth from "doctrines of demons" in occult realms which is contrary to the Word of God. Praise God that He is our merciful, all-powerful, forgiving, ever-loving Heavenly Father!

Forgiveness Is a Beauty Treatment

As Christian believers, members of the Body of Christ the Church of which Jesus is the Head, we need to turn away from all sinful thoughts and practices no matter how or when they occurred. The Scriptural way to do this is to repent and confess them as sins against God so that He can give us "a new heart and new Spirit" (Ezek. 18:30-32). We need to follow the Lord's warnings through the prophet: "turn and live" (vs. 32). God does not desire our spiritual death from such causes: He wants us to live in the Power of the Holy Spirit. In our own human power, we cannot turn away from sinful habit patterns and addictions of the past (whether they are spiritual, mental, emotional or physical). But, by the Grace of God, because of what Jesus did for us when He paid the price for our sins and took them upon Himself at Calvary, you and I can with repentant hearts confess these sins, accept God's forgiveness and the cleansing Power of the Blood of Jesus. He sets us captives free and gives us sight where we are (and have long been) blind. He opens prison doors so that we can walk out into His glorious liberty (not the world's license) and LIVE in the joyous Power of His Holy Spirit! In Ephesians 1:7 (NEB) we read: "In Christ our release is secured and our sins are forgiven through the shedding of His blood." We can become "FREED TO LIVE."

This is the message I had preached at a Saturday night Healing Service in a Church recently. A few weeks later, I received this moving testimony to the "beauty of holiness"—from a stranger who visited that night and responded to the Lord's call to forgiveness—not only for herself but for others. With her permission, I quote from her letter:

"I have been divorced for fifteen years. My ex-husband married my best friend who was the church secretary. We were all in church every time the doors were open. I raised three children who were 9, 11, and 15 years old at the time he left us. All these fifteen years I had held on to hate, bitterness, and resentment for him and for her, of course. I tried to turn my children against both of them. It worked, I thought, for several years.

"I must tell you what happened at your Mission the Saturday night of my healing at the altar ministry. You were busy with someone else—so I went to the minister and his wife and cried as I told them how I hated both my ex-husband and his wife. They made me say their names as they prayed for healing of bitterness, etc. When I left the church service I felt wonderful, so light, like walking on air! I attended every session, even Sunday School. The whole weekend was wonderful and I read all three of your books!

"Let me tell you what happened a month later when my last daughter was married. Her father and his wife had planned and paid for the whole wedding. I was like an invited guest—which I thought I could handle until . . . After the ceremony, all the guests had left for the reception and my ex-husband and his wife and my children and their spouses were in the back of the church. He said something ugly and I gave it right back to him. Then all of us went to the reception. It was so hard trying to pretend! When all the guests had left the reception except for our family, I told my daughter I was sorry for talking so ugly to her father. She and I embraced and both of us cried a lot of tears. Then I went up to his wife, embraced her and asked her forgiveness—and she asked my forgiveness for all the hurt she had caused us. We forgave each other through our tears. Then I went to my ex-husband and asked his forgiveness for hating him all these years and making the children hate him. He asked my forgiveness for not being a good husband. What a day that was! He has since written to me and said he was sorry for so many things that happened in our 18 years of marriage.

"Your Healing Mission really ministered to me. Thank God I've gotten rid of that load! Maybe now God will show me some direction in my life. Also, my children are so happy about us being able to talk—at last! God bless you and your work!"

NINE

THE CHRISTIAN FAMILY

*S*cripture has not changed its message—but over the past almost 2,000 years various cultures have not often heard it as it was originally proclaimed by Jesus and the Apostle Paul. When Jesus rescued the woman caught in adultery from the men who were about to stone her, a new attitude toward women came into being. Many of the accounts of Luke's Gospel stress our concern for the deplorable position of women (often hardly more than slaves) in those days.

In Paul's letters to the Ephesians and the Colossians, he spelled out a very different picture from the customs of the day in which he wrote. In Ephesians 5:21, Paul admonished his readers: "Be subject to one another out of reverence for Christ." Then he addressed the wives: "be subject to your husbands, *as to the Lord*"—quite a different focus from the contemporary attitude of his day (italics mine). Paul then elaborated that the headship of the husband to his wife is to be like that of Christ as "the head of the Church, his body." In vs. 23, this comparison is clarified even more: "As the church is subject to Christ, so let wives also be subject in everything to their husbands." This analogy implies that as

Christ is the Protector and Provider in His relationship with the Church, so the husband as the "head of his wife" should have similar concern for her well-being — even as the wife is to be concerned with pleasing her husband. The Church as the Body of Christ is not to be pulling away from His Headship — so this analogy helps us to see the unity that is necessary in the wife's relationship with her husband in the Christian family.

Paul then brought a beautiful balance into his teaching by carefully cautioning the husbands: "love your wives, as Christ loved the church and gave himself up for her" (vs. 25). For a husband to fulfill the type that Paul described would be impossible without the headship of Jesus Christ in him. Then Paul continued in his description of the Christian husband: "Even so husbands should love their wives as their own bodies. He who loves his wife loves himself . . . For no man ever hates his own flesh, but nourishes and cherishes it, as Christ does the church, because we are members of his body" (vs. 28-30). After discussing the need for the husband "to leave his father and mother and be joined to his wife," Paul ended with this important summary: "let each one of you love his wife as himself, and let the wife see that she respects her husband" (vs. 33).

In writing to the Colossians, Paul elaborated further on Christian husband/wife relationships by saying: "Wives, be subject to your husbands, as is fitting in the Lord. Husbands, love your wives, and do not be harsh with them" (3:18-19). The picture given of the wife being subject to her husband as to the Lord's approval clarifies the relationship as "submission" — but not submersion! The Christian husband is portrayed here as being loving to his wife (as to his own body) and is specifically admonished against being harsh — no tyrant picture here! Love is the theme of this description of order in the home as Paul portrayed it. Here it may be helpful to read I Corinthians 13 — Paul's eloquent definition of love.

Peter, in his First Epistle, brought further emphasis on the wife being submissive to her husband and referred to Sarah's obedience to Abraham as her lord. The apostle described beautifully the Christian wife as one who would win her husband to the Lord by her "gentle and quiet spirit," her "reverent and chaste behavior" (3:1-6). Then he addressed the husbands: "Likewise you husbands, live considerately with your wives, bestowing honor on the woman as the weaker sex, since you are joint heirs of the grace of life" (3:7). And, having created the picture of a considerate husband who honors his wife, Peter added words of extra incentive: "in order that your prayers may not be hindered!" These words imply that God will not be pleased by the husband who dishonors his wife and treats her in an unloving or cruel way. Male chauvinism is not condoned here.

Paul declared thus the principle of headship in writing his First Letter to the Corinthians: "But I want you to understand that the head of every man is Christ, the head of the woman is her husband, and the head of Christ is God" (11:3). This is the divine order in the home and it clearly emphasizes the importance of the Lordship of Jesus Christ in the husband. Obviously, this foundation is what makes the difference in relationships with the children. In many homes today, the children are the head—not the husband—and this disorder is strictly unwise and unscriptural. It creates monstrous problems in family relationships when the Biblical authority principle is turned upside down!

Now let us look at this matter in a practical way. For example, if you, dear reader, are a wife, the Lord may be trying to show you some specific ways He wants you to change your relationship with your husband. Are you willing to listen to His Holy Spirit? Is jealousy of your husband one of those nagging sins you don't want to admit? Do you allow yourself to feel neglected—working up a real "pity-party"? Or do you thank God that your husband is not an irresponsible man who can't hold down a good job? Do you grumble and complain when he is late coming home from work? Do you spoil with your nagging, sulky looks and whining voice the good dinner that you spent considerable time and money preparing? If so, you are fulfilling the old adage about "the cow that gave a good bucket of milk and kicked it over!"

Do you *really* listen to your husband—*creatively*, sensing the inner wounds in his spirit as a result of his day's conflicts and pressures? Will you try to put yourself in his place— being concerned about *his* needs when he opens the door? Do you really welcome him as "God's gift to you"—or do you hasten to dump your day's problems on him before he can even remove his coat? The day's pressures at work, and the traffic jams on the way home, have not exactly prepared him to be sympathetic until after he can catch his breath. Why not tell him how much you've missed him and leave the details of the children's ailments, escapades and crises till after dinner? It might save him from having stomach ulcers some day!

Have you ever thought that you (as a woman) were called to be a "Corner Pillar"? A corner pillar is a very important stone because it gives support to the building in which it is placed. In Psalms 144:12 we read: "that our daughters may be as corner pillars cut for the structure of a palace." In each home the wife is called to be "the corner pillar," lending support to her husband and to their children so that each one can better fulfil his or her special place in that "palace." She notices their needs and finds fulfillment in seeing them met through her. The bride united to her husband in loving respect becomes one with him spiritually and mentally—as well as physically. The call to "become one flesh" is far more than the one-ness of sexual intimacy: it is the one-ness of their mutual purpose to build a relationship that will grow in beauty and strength over the years. No wonder that the Bible warns: "Do not be mismated with unbelievers" (II Cor. 6:14). Marriage has a holy purpose and it requires the holiness of God to make it a crown of blessing to the man and woman who accept their union as a call in life to be fulfilled: in mutual, self-giving, sharing love. "Unless the Lord builds the house, those who build it labor in vain" (Ps. 127:1a).

A marriage built on lust and selfishness will be based on quicksand. When one tires sexually of the other, the marriage will probably sink into the abyss of failure. A marriage built on the illusion that "each one can do his (or her) own thing" is like a boat headed for dangerous shoals in stormy seas. A marriage that is riddled with laziness and self-concern on the part of the wife will collapse as the "corner pillar" can serve her purpose only if her desire is to help support and lend spiritual strength to the fulfillment of her mate's purpose — as well as to their children's needs. This does not mean that she is to be a doormat to be walked over and trampled upon in selfish dis-respect! A "corner pillar" is polished to become a beautiful, structural, functional source of strength. It does not move away from the relationship to the other "living stones" with which it is placed. A "corner pillar" submits to the authority of the Master Builder and fulfills as great a purpose as the stones it serves to hold together — even though some of them may be larger and more impressive.

Although the husband in the Christian family is called by God to be the head (as Christ is Head in him) it does not mean that he is to be arrogant in his relationship with his wife and children. How often as VMTC Prayer Counselors we have seen that a bad relationship with the earthly father usually distorts a child's relationship with his Heavenly Father. If the earthly father has not expressed love, the child usually grows up with an inability to accept the Heavenly Father's Love. How often we hear the adult's voice expressing the wistfulness of the child within him: "I know that my father must have loved me — but he *never* told me so." Sometimes that uneasy sense of rejection is voiced as: "My father was too busy making money! He never had time for me." As you can probably guess, the grown man cannot believe that God the Father has time for him either. Of course, if the father is a tyrant and only a nominal Christian, (or perhaps not a Christian at all) the example he sets for his children will make it very hard for them to accept God's Love. It is certainly true that children are to "obey their parents in the Lord, for this is right. 'Honor your father and mother' " (Eph. 6:1, 2). But, Paul also admonished: "Fathers, do not provoke your children to anger, but bring them up in the discipline and instruction of the Lord" (vs. 4). A cruel, angry father is usually the reason for rebellion in a person's life—sometimes repressed but revealed in silent procrastination. It is much harder for the children in a home where the father was an alcoholic or an unjust task-master, to grow up with a healthy faith in God. If the father disparages his wife for going to Church or "becoming religious," he can easily quench his children's faith. The sons in such a family are more apt to become rebellious teenagers. After all, they learned disrespect of God from their father's sneers. The daughters in such a family have a poor "role-model" in choosing later on their husbands: they will be sure that "religion doesn't really matter" and choose the wrong type of mate! Whereas, if the father sets the example in the home of showing love and respect for his wife, his daughters will subconsciously seek husbands like him. His sons will probably be more careful that the wives they choose will have some of the fine qualities of their mother. Most fathers are unaware of the fact that the greatest gift they can give to their children is the gift of a Christian home!

Some husbands who marry Christian wives begin to resent Jesus as if he were a rival lover. To be jealous of Jesus is a very common mistake made by couples. In such cases, it is most important for the Christian wife to win her husband by the fruit of the Spirit being borne in her life: to live the Love of Jesus—not preach at her husband about it! All too often, the wife flaunts her new priorities when she accepts Jesus as her Savior—so that her husband feels "closed out." His lack of understanding hardens into a rebellion against comprehending what she tells him of her new relationship with Jesus. If she neglects his needs because of her new ardor for Bible classes and Prayer Groups, the separation only becomes worse! Her husband may actually be thinking: "What's in this for me? I want my wife for myself. I don't want to share her with anybody!" The same thing can happen in a wife when her husband neglects her because she is not "spiritual enough"!

One of the greatest needs in the Church today is for a vital Men's Group where the vibrant witness of committed younger men can reach out to those disturbed husbands who can hear the "Good News" better from other men whom they respect and admire as peers in the community. Most men find it harder to come to a living faith in Jesus if their wives have found this Reality first and are "pushing it at them." The wife who is so eager for God to change her husband needs to be *even more* eager for Him to change her first! If she suddenly stops doing the thing that she knows has been a bone of contention, her husband will in time take note of it. For example, if being late and keeping him waiting, is the wife's form of passive rebellion, her new punctuality will begin to get his attention. Scripture verses pinned to his pillow may please some husbands but it is more apt to anger those who already feel that their wives are neglecting them to become "super-spiritual." A change of heart—becoming more thoughtful and loving—is a better way. After all, the most important sign of receiving the Baptism in the Holy Spirit is not "speaking in tongues" (although that is certainly an important gift)—but rather the changed life! The wife can be changed to be a joyous surprise to her husband! If she welcomes her husband's sexual advances instead of hiding behind tiredness or vague excuses, he will begin to take note of this. The wife does not need to become gimmicky and meet her husband at the door in a "see-through" black nightgown! He will know the difference when her heart (not just her body) is responding to his love-making. If the wife is *really* "super-spiritual," her everyday life with her husband will bear the fruit of love in such a meaningful way that he will probably become curious to find what she has found—this new Reality in her life (the Love of Jesus) will become such a blessing to him that he will be open to experience it for himself.

How often we have seen in VMTC Prayer Counseling that when the wife really changes in her attitudes to her husband and children, this evokes a desire in the husband to receive the same ministry. Even if he does not respond quickly, the new freedom in the wife's life will enable her to be more fully God's channel of forgiving, unselfish love to her whole family. She will be freed from the fear of past confrontations and thus be better able to resolve future ones in the Love of Jesus. If the wife really ministers to her family "as unto the Lord" there will be new Peace in the home. She will not manipulate to get her own way—nor be jealous of her children's love for their father. She will be the peacemaker as the Lord guides her—not out of fear.

The Amplified Translation of I Thessalonians 5:17 stresses: "Be unceasing in prayer" which means that we are to pray with faith and perseverance. In II Thessalonians 2:17, Paul admonishes his readers to keep their hearts unswerving, to be steadfast in the Lord—in spite of the uncertainties and problems of life. Husbands who have the humility to hear the Lord through their wives will be doubly blessed as they face together in prayer the crises and decisions in life. God can and often does speak through the wife who is committed not just to hear but to *be* His Will. The Pilgrim men who sailed on the Mayflower all carried in their pockets a card which said: "The way to prosper is to love and serve God." Some Christian men today carry in their pockets a small cross to remind them that He is the Lord of their lives, including their wallets! The husband who is generous with his wife shows his love for her by not demeaning her with his stinginess. But, the greatest gift a husband can give his wife is not monetary: it is the gift of understanding! Remembering her birthday and their wedding anniversary does not require great sums of money—it requires thoughtfulness on his part. Telling her he loves her (even if the meal was a flop) will assuage her sense of guilt. If he takes a minute to compliment her cooking, she will be encouraged to become a good cook. Appreciation of each other will do much to heal past, nagging criticisms of each other in a family where the Love of Jesus becomes newly evident. As each one comes closer to Jesus, the result will be that His Love will draw them closer to each other.

It has been rightly said that the child is blessed if he has someone to believe in him so that in this level of trust he can bring out his problems honestly—unafraid of snap, unjust judgments or mocking teasing. In a Christian family, there should be no partiality. If a parent feels partial to one child, it is urgent that prayer change such an un-God-like attitude. Perhaps the difficult child needs more attention: children need a parent who realizes that their griefs are real and require understanding sympathy—even though from the adult perspective the problem may seem trivial and passing. Each child needs to know that his/her efforts to achieve in life will be met with merited, loving appreciation. It is damaging if the parent moves the goal farther after the child has eagerly worked to fulfill it, as a sense of injustice and resulting bitterness are thus provoked by the parent who is never satisfied, always demanding more. The child in a Christian family needs to learn unselfishness through wise, consistent discipline but also through prayer and kindly commendation. Both parents need to spend time with their children in "the Family Altar" but also in "the Family Conference" where prayer and priorities can be shared to give each member a sense of acceptance in the home as well as to encourage their need to accept Jesus as Savior.

Sadly enough, some marriages reach a point of no return. Usually, divorce does not really solve problems because it creates more problems! Jesus gave some important guidelines but they are not always heeded today—even by Christian couples: "whoever divorces his wife, except for unchastity, and marries another, commits adultery" (Matt. 19:9). Jesus pointed to the sin of thoughts of lust by saying: "everyone who looks at a woman lustfully has already committed adultery with her in his heart" (Matt. 5:28). In our permissive society, the divorce rate is ever increasing and many are the victims of the sins of their partners (and often of the courts who make divorce too easy). Paul wrote: "But, if the unbelieving partner desires to depart, let it be so; in such a case the brother or sister is not bound. For God has called us to peace. Wife, how do you know whether you will save your husband? Husband, how do you know whether you will save your wife" (I Cor. 7:15-16)? How few heed this Scripture today!

Not only during the time of the divorce process but also during the years that follow, the children are badly hurt by this disruption of family life. Most children take the blame on themselves and feel confused by divided loyalties. The single parent faces horrendous problems which require the wisdom of the Lord to solve. The rejection felt by the injured spouse can only really be healed by the love of Jesus. The need to forgive the offending partner—even till seventy times seven—is very real so that bitterness will not corrode the newly reconstructed home that has lost one of its pillars and now lacks the unity of two parents in agreement. The legal and financial aspects are often devastating but the emotional wounds are even greater. The loneliness and bitterness, the inadequacy and fears of the future can only be healed by the Love of Jesus. The weight of a single parent's responsibility can only be borne by the Lord Himself who promised the believer to be with him (or her) always (Matt. 28:20). VMTC Prayer Counseling has helped many single parents to regain their stability so that they can re-build with their children the shattered fabric of their home, shoring up the foundations with the help of Christian brothers and sisters in the Church as the Family of God.

In one case, a 40 year old woman was shocked to find that her husband was going to divorce her to marry her best friend. As the husband was a prominent doctor in a small town, this shame was all the more painful — but the mother's real concern was not so much for herself as for their three teenage sons who were very angry with their father. They felt not only bitter because of his betrayal of their mother but also rejected because (for the sake of the "other woman") he was callously destroying their home. During the time of our Prayer Counseling ministry, the wife was healed of her feelings of rejection as well as anger, jealousy, fear of the future and self-pity at the destruction of their home. It was hardest to forgive her husband because of what he was doing to their sons in his infatuation for her former friend. When this mother's Prayer Counseling session was ended, she had been able to forgive the offending husband as an act of her will — and God's Love poured into her heart to make the act of forgiving a reality as the Peace of God took away her fears! The future had not changed: she would have to see her former friend enjoying the companionship and financial comforts that had been rightfully hers until her husband allowed temptation to become sin and destroy their marriage. But, *she had changed*! The rejected wife was no longer rejected! She had been healed by the Love of Jesus and the amazing grace that she had experienced in those few hours made her able to trust God for the future. Soon with the help of their Church, she and her sons were able to stabilize their home under the Lordship of Jesus. God has promised in His Word to be the husband to the widow and the father to the orphans (Is. 54:4-5 and Ps. 68:5). Praise God — for in overcoming what Satan intended for evil, He brought Victory. This tragedy in family life brought her much closer to her sons but more importantly each one came into a living experience with Jesus as Lord of their lives. Their Church gave them the needed support in the community and each one found fulfillment in the Body of Christ as a vital reality—not a duty, but a call to deeper commitment to the One who made this healing a reality!

TEN

THE CHURCH AS THE BRIDE OF CHRIST

*A*s we have seen in looking at the Biblical foundation for the Christian family, it is to be the "little church" within the Church. Paul repeatedly refers to the relationship between Christ and His Church as a type for the husband's relationship to his wife. The sacrificial love of Jesus for the Church is likened to the love that the Christian husband will have for his wife if he accepts fully the Headship of Jesus as Lord. As Christ is the Protector of the Church, so the husband is to be the protector of his family. As Christ is the Provider for the Church, so the husband is to be the provider for his family. Christ gave himself up for the Church "that he might present the church to himself in splendor, without spot or wrinkle or any such thing, that she might be holy and without blemish" (Eph. 5:27).

The Church is not to be dominated by various competitive groups of people but to led in unity by the Holy Spirit so that the love of Jesus is the motivating factor. As a loving wife is eager for people to meet and know her husband, so the Church as the Bride must continually yearn for people to meet Jesus in a close personal way. The purpose of the Bride is to make Christ known to others — not to raise money for good projects but to share His Love with those who need to know Him as their personal Savior. When Church members leave at the end of a service, their contagious joy of worship can carry them out into the "mission field"—the world about them! Secular humanism creeps into the Church to lure the Bride to desert her first Love. The world with its self-pleasing is constantly tempting the Bride to turn her eyes on "What can I get out of the Church?" instead of living out "What have I to give to my Lord?" Actually, the only thing we have to give to God is ourselves—and this we need to do because He created us with freedom of will! A bride can give her husband many presents—but the gift that he really wants is the gift of herself. Even so, Jesus calls us (as members of the Bride) *to give ourselves*—not just a tip on Sunday morning—but to give our lives wholeheartedly to Him so that abiding in union with Him, we can fulfill our purpose as His Bride. We are the Church—all of us—not just the pastors or priests!

Distractions and temptations come to the Church because it is made up of imperfect human beings who are subjected by the enemy to pressures intended to take our eyes off Jesus. Materialism, the lust of the eyes and pride can divide the Church and distort its true vision of being a servant Church. When the pride of life with its self-exaltation infects the Church's blood stream, Jesus can no longer be Lord and His Purposes to redeem the world can no longer be fulfilled through His Bride's ministry. Pastor David Wilkerson wrote in his challenging book, SET THE TRUMPET TO THY MOUTH, that at one time he lost the Lord's true vision and began to build a materialistic "Kingdom." Then God spoke to him and restored the original call to minister to the street people on drugs in New York—to return to his first vision—and since then he has built a dynamic Church in Times Square!

How easy it is for the enemy to sow tares in the field of wheat as Jesus remarked in a parable about the Kingdom of Heaven. We are reminded that this is the way it will be at the close of the age: "The son of man will send his angels, and they will gather out of his Kingdom all causes of sin and all evildoers, and throw them into the furnace of fire; there men will weep and gnash their teeth. Then the righteous will shine like the sun in the Kingdom of their Father. He who has ears, let him hear" (Matt. 13:41-43). Does the Church need to heed this warning today? The Bridegroom is calling His Bride to be "without spot or blemish" (Eph. 5:27). Are we the Bride willing to let God circumcise our hearts to remove the sinful lusts of the flesh and the coveting of the eyes that are so characteristic of the world's lifestyle? How can we, the Bride, be given to the Bridegroom if we are infected by the same disease called "the pride of life" that is crippling the world today? Most Christians, although Church-goers, seem to be ignorant of the danger of a "worldly spirit" and their life-styles are so like those of the world that the reaper would have a difficult time sorting out the wheat from the tares. Church-going is more like attending a religious club — and responsibility to the Bridegroom seems not to figure in the thinking of so many because they are apparently not even aware that they are called to be the Bride of Christ — and that He will return to claim His Bride! When He does, will we be the wheat — or the tares? In the end, the good will be separated from the bad for all eternity!

In the Church today, we seem to have three kinds of people. There are those who are sure: "It can't be done." Then there are those who say; "It ought to be done and somebody else ought to be doing it." And then there are those who are doing it! Doing what? Bringing in the Kingdom, of course! When Jesus called His disciples, He said "Come" — but later He said, "Go!" Too many today are saying in actuality: "Here am I, Lord. Send my brother." Jesus has called you and me to receive the Good News so that *we* can become those who communicate this to others. It's not enough to *know* the Word of God intellectually! Unless you and I can communicate what we believe to others, we are missing the purpose of the Divine Commission. Someone has said that the longest distance is between our head and our heart! William Barclay in his commentary on the Gospel of Matthew wrote: "The Cross was not to be the end; it was to be the beginning of the unleashing of that power which was to surge throughout the whole world" (p. 156). Are we in the Church today unleashing that Power which Jesus made available to us through His Resurrection — and later through the sending of the Holy Spirit at Pentecost? Are we preparing for His return? He has given us the recipe for life and in every decision we make, you and I are given an opportunity: whether we will live for Him and give ourselves to be spent for others *or* whether we will live selfishly. A missionary once said: "The sad news is that there are not enough people carrying the Good News." All nations and all denominations, all ages and all ethnic groups are called to fulfill the Divine Commission. Paul responded to the call: "Come over into Macedonia and help us." For you, the call may be: "Come share the Love of Jesus with this helpless mother who is being victimized by a rebellious teenager." *Or*, "Come listen and pray with the woman who is in shock after being told by her husband of 25 years that he is casting her off like a worn-out garment!" *Or*, "Come pray with the man who has suddenly been told that his job has been terminated!" In the Church today we must become more than an institution: we must share our faith in Jesus, living out our love for Him in our every day relationships with others — not just in our own blood family but also in the larger Family-in-Christ that has been redeemed by His Blood! Are you willing to change your life style to make sure that someone receives the spiritual transfusion of His Love through you? Today?

There are two kinds of fasting: from food — and most of us would be healthier if the scales did not tip so heavily when we stood on them. But there is the fasting referred to in Isaiah 58:6-9: "Is not this the fast that I choose: to loose the bonds of wickedness, to undo the thongs of the yoke, to let the oppressed go free, and to break every yoke? Is it not to share your bread with the hungry, and bring the homeless poor into your house; when you see the naked, to cover him, and not to hide yourself from your own flesh? Then shall your light break forth like the dawn, and your healing shall spring up speedily; your righteousness shall go before you, the glory of the Lord shall be your rear guard. Then you shall call, and the Lord will answer; you shall cry, and he will say, Here I am."

The fast God has set for us may be to deny our self-will: to go against our own feelings. We need to discern between our needs and our greeds! A wise man once said: "There are no pockets in a shroud"—we can't take it with us! About half of the parables of Jesus deal with money or wealth—in fact, someone has counted over 750 passages in the Bible where money is mentioned! If every person in the Church tithed, there would be ample funds to meet all its needs. Do you trust God enough to release to Him (without fear) *anything He asks of you*—including that Biblical ten percent? He never fails those of us who have made this commitment. Why not join the "Tithers' Club" instead of the Country Club? Someone has said that when the devil whispers to you, "What if . . . ?" you and I can shout back at him "So what!" If our Heavenly Father is our Source of supply, then we will not be worried over dire predictions about the economy. Jesus said: ". . . give and it will be given unto you; good measure, pressed down, shaken together, running over, will be put into your lap" (Luke 6:38). Paul wrote in his Second Letter to the Corinthians: "The point is this: he who sows sparingly will also reap sparingly, and he who sows bountifully will also reap bountifully" (9:6). What is the Holy Spirit saying to you about your giving—NOW?

God is calling His Church to a *new obedience* to His Word —to see Christianity as the *revelation of His Purposes, not a watered down speculation about the Bible*! We need to repent of the sins that have kept us from being the Bride without blemish: for our sins are an offense to God. This means that repentance is to be our life-style, not just a one-time act at conversion. It must be *a new life lived in Christ Jesus*! The Church needs to be evangelized—brought to the living awareness of the relevance of the Good News of Jesus Christ in today's world with its mounting problems and constant changes. The Church as the Bride of Christ needs to reveal His forgiveness and His unchanging Love—*His faithfulness in the midst of the faithlessness of humanistic morals and worldly solutions*! "Jesus Christ is the same, yesterday, today and forever" (Heb. 13:8). As we the Church proclaim this by the witness of our lives which are lived in the midst of conflict with the evil one, we can become part of the answer because *Jesus is the Answer*! He has a plan and a place for *each one* of us in this confused world today. As we the Church, the Body of which He is the Head, yield ourselves to reveal His forgiving Love and His empowering Spirit we can speak to those who are dangerously, alas, seeking supernatural power in Satan's kingdom. We can proclaim to a dying world that wonderful gift of salvation which is "wholeness for living" as well as "eternity in heaven." In His Grace, we become FREED TO LIVE!

There are in the Church today many who discount the Second Coming of Jesus. There are others who set a date and make prophecy a trip in itself—although Jesus warned that not even the angels would know the day and the hour of His return (Matt. 24:36)! The Bible has been said to be one-third prophetic—and many of these Scriptures have already been fulfilled, especially concerning the restoration of Israel as a nation. Until Jesus returns, we are called to live expectantly—like the wise virgins who had trimmed their wicks and filled their lamps with oil (Matt. 25:1-13). We need not be put off by the extremists who are always setting a date—seemingly demanding Jesus' immediate return. The Rapture of the Church *will* take place! Whether it will be before or after the Tribulation, no one can categorically say although many try to prove their divergent theories. Jesus came in fulfillment of prophecy and He gave us prophecies concerning "end times." Rightly used, prophecy helps us to be patient as we wait for the Lord's return. It enables us to see in better prospective the Hitlers and Khadafys and Khomenis! Prophecy puts the Church in perspective because we are called to be the "Bride of Christ"—*forever*! It helps us to remember that *we need to live in readiness*—our lives prepared to meet Christ face to face! Even so, "Come Lord Jesus!" (Rev. 22:20)

This prophecy was given to me by the Lord as I was about to teach on "Total Commitment" at a VMTC Clergy School of Prayer Counseling in June, 1987. It was printed in the booklet "Expectations for a New Decade" published by the Episcopal Church Renewal Ministries for the July '87 Congress on the Holy Spirit and World Evangelization held in New Orleans. May these words speak to your hearts today as they re-affirm II Chronicles 7:14: "Repent and come apart from your sins of the spirit and of the flesh—and from the humanism which infiltrates and tarnishes your Ministry. Set your hearts and your priorities on Me so that I may strengthen you to turn away from these sins and stand against the deceits and temptations of the world, the flesh and the devil. Pray in My Spirit for *a new call to holiness* so that the money-changers can be cast out and My people will be taught to respond to My call to Total Commitment—to depend on Me and seek to *know My Voice* amid the clamor of false prophets. When My Church becomes purified to be truly My Bride, I will return and call her to Myself. Glorify Me, your Lord and Master, for that is Who I am—not your 'Cosmic Bell-Hop.' I love you! You are My Body—but your sins have made a separation between you and Me. Turn away from your idolatries and your double-mindedness, from your rebellion against Me and My priorities on your lives. Repent and turn away from these wicked ways. Turn and *live* in the Power of My Spirit. The abundant life does not consist of things but *in My Presence you will know the abundance of My Love!*"

APPENDIX

by

The Rev. Dr. Alfred L. Salt, D. Min.
M.A., B.D., A.M.P. (Harvard Business School)

INTRODUCTION

THE NATURE AND SCOPE OF VMTC PRAYER COUNSELING

*I*n the spring of 1981 I was sharing in a Healing Mission where I had gone to hear Anne S. White, President of Victorious Ministry Through Christ (VMTC) speak on the "Healing of Relationships." The Vicar had invited me to assist in the Laying-on of hands for the healing of those who would come forward, following the concluding address of that day. I was asked to work with Anne White at the altar rail. That conference and that experience of sharing with her was my first introduction to the Victorious Ministry Through Christ.

When, later on, she invited me to register for the forthcoming Clergy School of Prayer Counseling, it was a surprise and yet it was not. I had become active in the healing ministry through the Order of St. Luke, first, as an associate member and then as chaplain. I had shared in numerous healing conferences and had fresh memories of two 2 week healing missions in Jamaica in the West Indies. I had experienced the Lord's blessings through all of these occasions.

Since that initial experience at my first Prayer Counseling School, I have become more and more deeply involved in the work of VMTC. I completed the number of Schools necessary to be released as a lead Prayer Counselor, and later was asked to be a staff member, and then a coordinator of a local School. Since 1986, I have been a Director on the U.S. National Board with the responsibility of directing two Schools a year. In 1987, I was elected to the International Board of Directors which coordinates the work of VMTC in several countries, including Australia, Canada, Finland and Pakistan. In the latter, we are presently establishing a Prayer Counseling ministry with both the blessing and participation of the Rt. Rev. Arne Rudvin, the Bishop of Karachi in the Church of Pakistan. In September 1987, along with my wife Betty and the Rev. Barry Skellett of Australia and his wife, Dr. Helen Skellett, I made my second visit to Pakistan to assist with the directing of their fourth School.

This appendix is adapted from part of my doctoral program in Anglican-Lutheran-Roman Catholic dialogue. It speaks to both the interdenominational aspect of VMTC (for its participants include Christians of many and varied denominations) and also to the international co-operation among Christians of many different backgrounds coming together under the headship of Jesus Christ.

The Rev. Dr. Alfred L. Salt, *Rector*
All Saints' Church
Millington, New Jersey
November, 1987

ONE

THE MINISTRY DEFINED

*W*hat is Prayer Counseling as defined by *Victorious Ministry Through Christ?* The invitation form expresses this:

"A Training School for ministers called to the care of people who need healing of brokenness and bondages caused by crippling relationships or circumstances of the past. During the three days of the School, the Lord sets His ministers free from their own blocks and bondages. As they share more fully in His Victory of the Cross, they can claim more effectively Jesus' power over sin and Satan in the lives of their people. This is not a new psychological, counseling technique. It is loving, listening and believing prayer. The person in need of counseling may be a victim of (1) the sins of others, in childhood or in the more recent past of marriage relationships; (2) his own sins, many of which he cannot truly identify; (3) the very real attacks of Satan, especially through occult involvement today or in the past. The Holy Spirit releases His supernatural gifts of wisdom, knowledge, discernment, faith, healing, etc. through trained counselors who are 'two in agreement' for this healing. The minister-trainee is taught through Scripture and practice-work how to be the

Lord's instrument for His Victorious Ministry to the broken and sin-sick world about him. It is essential that he be willing to be healed himself first. This is not a 'rehabilitation center,' but a Training School for those called by God to help others. Trainees must attend at least 3 Schools before being given recognition as VMTC Prayer Counselors."

Who may participate? Again as the invitation states: "This School is for ordained ministers with a pastoral charge over a congregation. Only 30 applications can be accepted. This limited size allows each person to have a private four-hour Prayer Counseling appointment. It also provides the opportunity for each one to begin training by 'backing up' experienced team members in these appointments. Wives are urged to attend (unless they are pregnant). Children are not admitted.

"A few well qualified, stable, mature lay people may come if their pastor has already attended at least 1 School. Applications must be accompanied by a letter of recommendation by this pastor under whose authority and direction they must work. Obviously, it would be preferable for the pastor to have completed at least 2 Schools before the lay people are graduated — if he is not able to complete the 4 Schools himself. Acceptance is subject to approval by Anne S. White, the Central Coordinator, after receiving a report that the applicants have been Prayer Counseled locally (wherever possible). This ensures better adjustment to the fast pace of the School."

TWO

THE MINISTRY: BASIC PRINCIPLES

*T*his ministry, appealing to Christians of various backgrounds, is built on the foundation of Scripture, prayer, confession of sin, absolution, forgiveness, freedom from bondage, deliverance and healing.

The Importance of Scripture

First of all, it is Scriptural. It is a ministry which takes Scripture and its promises seriously. Reflecting on this as an Episcopalian, it could be stated simply as the response asked of all who would be ordained into the ministry of the Church. "I do solemnly declare that I do believe the Holy Scripture of the Old and New Testaments to be the Word of God, and to contain all things necessary to salvation." (THE BOOK OF COMMON PRAYER, Ordination to the Priesthood, p. 526) Quoting from my article in May 1987 issue of *Sharing*, a journal of Christian Healing:

" 'Salvation' (from the Greek 'SOZO'—to save, to keep from harm, preserve, rescue) implies a rescuing action. In the DICTIONARY OF NEW TESTAMENT THEOLOGY, the author of the article on Redemption points out: 'Whenever men by their own fault or through some superior power have come under the control of someone else and have lost their freedom to implement their will and decision, and when their own resources are inadequate to deal with the other power, they can regain their freedom only by the intervention of a "third party." ' It is in the light of this need of a 'third party' that Paul could write to the Galatians: 'It is for freedom that Christ has set us free. Stand firm, then, and do not let yourselves be burdened again by a yoke of slavery' (Gal. 5:1). The gospel message is a message of freedom, liberation in the right and proper sense. It is not freedom to do as you please, but freedom for each of us to respond to the perfect will of God in Christ Jesus."

The coming together of Anglicans, Lutherans and Roman Catholics as well as those from other denominations and trans-denominational churches must be built upon a firm foundation of Scripture. The wholeness, the completeness we seek can be discovered in and through Scripture. It is the Scriptural base that provides the "glue" so that Christians (from Assembly of God to Roman Catholic) can be bound together in a mosaic that is more beautiful than its parts and yet would not be a mosaic without its parts.

The Importance of Prayer

Secondly, I would say that the strength and "success" of VMTC Prayer Counseling lies in its commitment to prayer. In Jesus' discourse on prayer, He exhorts: "And I tell you, ask, and it will be given to you; seek, and you will find; knock, and it will be opened to you. For every one who asks receives; and he who seeks finds, and to him who knocks it will be opened" (Luke 11:9-13). It brings to mind that passage from "Mort d'Arthur" by Alfred Tennyson which speaks to the truth of Scripture: "More things are wrought by prayer than this world dreams of" (line 414). In an ecumenical ministry we are called upon to pray. If we are to be His disciples we need to be a praying people. Martin Luther once said (recorded in his TISHREDE): "I have twice as much to do today and therefore I need to pray twice as long." Prayer Counseling is built, as its name indicates, upon prayer: praying for guidance, praying for direction, praying for spiritual discernment and praying for the outpouring of the Holy Spirit.

The Importance of the Holy Spirit

This leads to the third source of strength for this ecumenical ministry of VMTC Prayer Counseling: a belief in and a waiting upon the Holy Spirit for guidance and direction. Again, returning to that passage in Luke, Jesus concluded His discourse on prayer by saying: "If you then, who are evil, know how to give good gifts to your children, how much more will the heavenly Father give the Holy Spirit to those who ask Him." Jesus tells us, as recorded in John 14:25, "But the Counselor, the Holy Spirit, whom the Father will send in my name, he will teach you all things, and bring to your remembrance all that I have said to you." In a Prayer Counseling session I once had with an Episcopal priest, he burst out: "I didn't tell you that about myself!" "No," I replied, "that is what this ministry is all about." If we believe in the gifts of the Spirit—wisdom, knowledge, discernment, faith, healing, miracles, tongues, interpretation of tongues, and prophecy—should we be surprised when God, in love, gives them to us? The Acts of the Apostles records what happens when Christians respond in the power of the Holy Spirit. Truly this is a strength of the Prayer Counseling Ministry.

The Importance of Confession of Sin

Having been involved for several years in an altar rail ministry of healing (by that I mean persons coming forward for the Laying-on of hands or the Anointing with oil) I realized both its strength and its weakness. Its strength lies in the fact that an individual as an act of faith comes forward believing that God can and does heal. Many can attest to the fact that God heals through this simple act of humility, combined with the Laying-on of hands or the Anointing with oil. Its weakness lies in the fact that the person seeking healing may not be getting to the heart of the issue. For example, on one occasion a doctor came forward during an "altar rail" ministry seeking healing for his arthritis, which had become active. In a moment of spiritual knowledge I was led to ask, "Who are you angry with?" The effect was an immediate awareness of the need for confession. Following confession of sin and absolution, it was then appropriate to continue with the laying-on of hands. The need for confession of sin was an essential part of the healing process. It is consistent with the exhortation of James in the fifth chapter, verse 16, "Therefore, confess your sins one to another, and pray one for another, that you may be healed."

The Importance of Absolution or Assurance of Pardon

As a priest, I believe that one of the great gifts that God has given to His Church is the power of absolution. As Jesus said to His apostles: "Receive the Holy Spirit. If you forgive the sins of any, they are forgiven; if you retain the sins of any, they are retained." This power comes from Jesus Himself. As John records in his Gospel: "He breathed on them" (John 20:22-23). In his first Epistle, John wrote: "If we say we have no sin, we deceive ourselves, and the truth is not in us. If we confess our sins, he is faithful and just, and will forgive our sins and cleanse us from all unrighteousness. If we say we have not sinned, we make him a liar, and his word is not in us" (1:8-10). On one occasion, having been invited to give the homily at a Healing Service in a nearby Presbyterian

The Ministry: Basic Principles

Church and to share in the Laying-on of hands and the Anointing with oil, a woman came forward for anointing. As she knelt there, with her specific requests, she was moved to make a confession of sin. As she completed her confession, I gave her the absolution in the name of Jesus Christ. In the background the organ had been playing. Suddenly, I became aware that the sound was not that of the organ but of a heavenly choir. The words of Scripture leapt into the forefront of my mind: "Just so, I tell you, there will be more joy in heaven over one sinner who repents than over ninety and nine righteous persons who need no repentance" (Luke 15:7).

The Prayer Counseling ministry would not be complete without both confession of sin and absolution, or, as non-liturgical churches would call it, "the assurance of pardon." The person being Prayer Counseled must acknowledge his sin, repent of it and ask for God's forgiveness. Without this, there can be no healing of relationships. As a priest, I was accustomed to making and hearing confession, and yet in my own first Prayer Counseling session I had to come to grips with the reality of confession in a new and different way. I had to confess my sins in the presence of my Prayer Counseling team, which was comprised of two men and a woman, none of whom were of my religious persuasion. It was at first both a humbling and a threatening experience. Through it, however, I learned in a deeper way the meaning of God's love. I had gained new insights into that beautiful gift Jesus had given to His Church.

It was this awareness of sin and the need to confess that led Anne S. White, the Founder and President of Victorious Ministry Through Christ, to begin her healing adventure. Her experience began in the loneliness of the middle of a long night as her son, then aged five, was in the midst of a severe asthmatic attack. In her own words from HEALING ADVENTURE, (p. 2):

"Thus began my healing adventure — an adventure with God, seeking to know more of His will; to practice more of the principles of prayer which our Lord taught in His earthly ministry; to follow Him. This has revolutionized my attitude toward God, toward my family and those about me. As a laywoman I have sought to be used to funnel His healing Love and Power into the lives of those whom He has brought into my life, not because I am worthy, but because He is worthy. I have seen His Love heal those bruised by the sin of the world; those filled with hate (as I once was); those victims of their own self-pity—the bitter, the fearful.

"This healing adventure which was begun over forty years ago has involved me in the ministry of intercessory prayer in many different countries as far apart as Japan, England, Singapore, Scandinavia, Pakistan, Canada and the Holy Land, as well as in many parts of America. Always our blessed Lord has revealed His healing Love. He is no respecter of persons, only conditions. The searching of the Scriptures has convinced me that in healing the sick, our Lord was proclaiming the Will of God; that it is a human 'No' rather more often than God's 'No.' To be divinely healed means to surrender to God. For many this price is too great, too costly. For many it is too hard to break free from the coddling of illness and assume full responsibility for life once more. For many it is easier to take a pill than to give up a life-long habit, grudge, resentment or fear. But after having witnessed the miracles of the healing love of Christ in my own life and those with whom our Lord has led me to pray, I am convinced that when we as the Body of Christ, the Church, provide a real climate of faith, His touch will have its ancient power!

"Twenty-five hundred years ago Hippocrates so wisely suggested treating the whole man. Later Plato said that one ought not to neglect the healing of the soul when making the effort to cure the body. We can be thankful for doctors both in England and America who have many centuries later confirmed the interaction between spirit, mind and soul— the relationships exemplified by our Lord in His earthly ministry of healing. We can be especially grateful for those doctors who pray with their patients or meet regularly with pastors to share the healing work of ministering to the whole man. A study of their writings points to the important part played by human emotions on the body. It is hoped that this book will help to relate the approach of psychosomatic medicine to our Lord's healing ministry: that which is taking place today through His Body the Church as well as during the visible ministry of Jesus of Nazareth."

The Importance of Forgiveness

Anne S. White points to an important element in the act of confession of sin, i.e., the need to forgive. Jesus tells us: "forgive us our sins as we forgive those who sin against us" (Luke 11:4). Jesus exhorts His followers: "Take heed to yourselves; if your brother sins, rebuke him, and if he repents, forgive him; and if he sins against you seven times in a day, and turns to you seven times and says 'I repent' you must forgive him" (Luke 17:3-4). Again, with Peter who came to Jesus asking Him about forgiveness: "Lord, how often shall my brother sin against me, and I forgive him? As many as seven times?" Peter thought himself to be generous. Jesus replies, "I do not say to you seven times, but seventy times seven" (Matt. 18:21ff). Forgive! Forgive! Forgive!

A few weeks ago a woman in my parish was expressing her dismay over the people who had repaired their pool. Inefficiency, poor workmanship, excuses and lack of reliability made her angry. The anger increased until one day she realized it did not have any result in getting the task at hand done. The anger was hurting no one other than herself. She had to forgive. This speaks to an important spiritual truth in VMTC Prayer Counseling. It is not important what someone does to you. It is how you react that is important! That is what we have to deal with. I can forgive someone — not only that person who openly asks for my forgiveness but also the one who may be completely oblivious to the need to seek forgiveness. I can be set free, but I need to forgive and to seek forgiveness.

The Importance of Being Set Free from Bondages to Persons, Places, Things or Experiences

Many people live in bondages—bondages to experiences, places, people and things. This is what Anne White discovered in her relationship with her mother-in-law. It is only in Christ that we can be set free from bondage. As Paul wrote to the Galatians: "For freedom Christ has set us free; stand fast therefore, and do not submit again to a yoke of slavery" (5:1). I can relate to this because of my own personal experience. As a young boy, while at Scout camp, I almost drowned, or I thought I was drowning. In my enthusiasm and foolishness I had tried to swim beyond my depth. I suddenly found myself in an upright position and I did not know how to tread water. I went down twice before someone positioned a long pole over me and I grabbed it and was pulled into the raft. It was a terrifying experience, so much so that I was not able to become an Eagle Scout because I could not bring myself to do the swimming and lifesaving required. When at seventeen I enlisted in the service, I had to swim or be rejected for the Officers' Training Program. By sheer force of will I swam, but I never overcame the fear that was within me. I lived with this fear, until about three years ago when it came up in one of my own Prayer Counseling sessions. I dealt with it—I confessed the sin of fear, I was pardoned and cut free from the bondage to that experience. I was delivered from the fear of drowning! I did not realize how totally free I was until the next summer when, while swimming at the lake by our cottage, I suddenly realized the absence of fear. I still "respect" the water. I know of its dangers, but I no longer have that fearful spirit which had been with me ever since that childhood experience. Truly we can be set free from bondages to persons, places, things or experiences. There is no need to return to a yoke of slavery. Being set free from bondages is an essential part of the VMTC Prayer Counseling Ministry.

The Importance of Deliverance

As an Episcopal priest, for years I have said the prayer of absolution as contained in the Prayer Book (THE BOOK OF COMMON PRAYER, p. 332). It goes as follows:

"Almighty God, our Heavenly Father, who of his great mercy hath promised forgiveness of sins to all those who with hearty repentance and true faith turn unto him, have mercy upon you, pardon and deliver you from all your sins, confirm and strengthen you in all goodness, and bring you to everlasting life; through Jesus Christ our Lord. Amen." Pardon and *deliver* you. I had heard unkind things about deliverance ministries. Does not this belong to some extremist Pentecostal sects? Most certainly not to staid and proper Episcopalians! But for years I had said this prayer, in the prayer of absolution. Absolution involves being delivered!

As I related this to my own experience of near drowning and the subsequent fear that came over me, I realized that not only was I cut free from the bondage to that experience, but I also was delivered from the spirit of fear that had hounded me for those many years. Truly I had been set free!

The VMTC Prayer Counseling Ministry takes seriously this need, when necessary, to be delivered from whatever spirits — whether it be fear, anxiety, lust, etc. — which may be oppressing us. This can only be done in the power of the Holy Spirit, as we pray for the gift of discernment — the discerning of spirits. This truly is one of the gifts as Paul describes in 1 Corinthians 12. We recall that Jesus gave authority to His apostles over the unclean spirits. "And he called to him the twelve, and began to send them out two by two, and gave them authority over the unclean spirits" (Mark 6:7).

The Importance of Healing and Commitment

A healing prayer is always a part of the VMTC Prayer Counseling Ministry. I have discovered, however, that many people want a healing and not necessarily to be healed! To be healed means to be thoroughly cleansed, changed, renewed. When the woman was taken in adultery, Jesus said, "neither do I condemn you; go, and do not sin again" (John 8:11). A true healing brings about change. For the Christian, this change can be achieved only in a life that is lived in Jesus Christ. We are powerless to help ourselves. Prayer Counseling as described by VMTC is a commitment ministry, for the healer is none other than Jesus Christ, Himself, who said, "apart from me you can do nothing" (John 15:5). Commitment means a total surrender to Him.

HEALING ADVENTURE
A Classic on Divine Healing
Originally published by LOGOS
Revised Edition published by Sovereign World, Ltd.

By the Author of:
Dayspring

"The Christian Army, the Church, has often been guilty of attacking its own wounded. Anne S. White's inspiring book, HEALING ADVENTURE, presents a most helpful description of the means by which wounded warriors can be ministered to for wholeness and healing in the Body of Christ.". . . **Rev. Vernon Stoop, Jr., Sr. Pastor, Shepherd of the Hills, United Church of Christ, Bechtelsville, PA, and Secretary/Treasurer North American Renewal Services Committee.**

* * * * *

"My personal journey, along with that of Betty, my wife, has been renewed and deeply enriched through the ministry of Anne S. White and the Prayer Counseling of Victorious Ministry Through Christ, Inc. I heartily commend her Scriptural, balanced, effective ministry through books, especially HEALING ADVENTURE which is the basic book for this ministry — and its sequel, TRIAL BY FIRE. I also recommend a Teaching Mission on "The Healing of Relationships" (or a "Free to Live" Mission) to bring about renewal for you and for your church today.". . . **The Rev. Dr. Alfred L. Salt, M.A., B.D., D. Min., Rector, All Saints' Church, Millington, NJ.**

$4.95 plus postage

VICTORIOUS MINISTRY THROUGH CHRIST, INC.
P.O. BOX 1804 • WINTER PARK, FLORIDA 32790 • 407-657-4893

TRIAL BY FIRE

Another practical handbook offering valuable guidelines for the difficult aspects of our walk.

If you have passed from the "honeymoon stage" of your walk and have begun to experience the purging and pruning of the Lord, and have become aware of the reality of spiritual warfare . . . , this book is a must.

Missioner, Teacher, Counselor, Author of: *JESUS, All in All, Healing Adventure, Dayspring, The Transforming Power of God, Healing Devotions,* & *Study Adventure in Trial by Fire.*

ANNE S. WHITE has given 25 years of her life to a lay ministry of writing, counseling, teaching, speaking, and sharing Christ in Churches of other denominations as well as in her own Episcopal Church. Her extensive preparation and experience in the work of "prayer counseling" and ministry to the sick at heart have fitted her to speak with authority, particularly on "Divine Healing," "Spiritual Warfare," "Commitment," "The Lordship of Jesus Christ," and "The Baptism in the Holy Spirit."

As an ecumenical Episcopalian, Mrs. White rejoices at the opportunity to work with all fellow Christians to fulfill the Lord's commission: "Go preach the Kingdom, heal the sick." Her emphasis is on the need for healing of relationships, of sick minds, emotions, spirits and bodies; so that men may become whole in deeper commitment to Jesus Christ—their Lord, Saviour, Redeemer, Healer, and Baptizer. Her lay ministry has been protected, empowered and extended by the Lord through years of spiritual warfare—which have equipped her to write *Trial by Fire.*

$3.50 plus postage

Order from:
IMPACT BOOKS
137 W. Jefferson • Kirkwood, MO 63122

OR:
VICTORIOUS MINISTRY THROUGH CHRIST, INC.
P.O. BOX 1804 • WINTER PARK, FLORIDA 32790 • 407-657-4893

STUDY ADVENTURE FOR TRIAL BY FIRE
More Meat for Men — by Anne S. White and Don Vanzant

Using this STUDY ADVENTURE will make Anne's practical book, *Trial by Fire*, come alive for you in an even more effective way! Questions help to pinpoint valuable signposts for your Christian walk. After your "mountaintop experiences," learn *how* to "hold your victory" in spiritual warfare and how to *grow* in total commitment — in order to overcome Satan's attacks. As the Lord uses them to develop character in you, He brings good out of what the enemy intended for evil.

"Far too many Christians fail to walk in victory. They either 'perish for a lack of knowledge' or they 'fail to walk in the Light as He is in the Light.' Either the lack of information concerning the depth of the Christian faith or the failure to be persevering in the practice of Christian discipline is sufficient to destroy the average Christian. This *Study Adventure* for Anne White's book, *Trial by Fire* provides an adequate learning tool to impart the knowledge concerning the victorious life that wins over satanic forces that attempt to destroy us. It also provides the motivation that can lead us to disciplined victorious living. This teaching tool is an appropriate resource for instruction in spiritual warfare and Christ-like living. I heartily recommend the use of this 'Study Adventure'"
— **Rev. Vernon Stoop, Jr. Senior Pastor, Shepherd of the Hills, United Church of Christ, Bechtelsville, Pennsylvania.**

"I have used the *Study Adventure* for *Trial by Fire* by Anne S. White and Don Vanzant as a homework assignment for adult Confirmation Class. What a perfect vehicle to point to tools for victorious living through the 'Lordship of Jesus,' the 'Baptism in the Holy Spirit,' 'Spiritual Warfare,' 'Repentance,' and 'How to Pray with Power!' This workbook helps new and mature Christians in their discipleship with obtainable goals of understanding over a period of a few weeks. Coupled with Bible study and good doctrine courses, your members should gain the proper balance needed for victorious living in the world today." — **The Rev. Clifford Horvath, Rector, Church of the Resurrection, Miami, Florida.**

$1.95 plus postage   ISBN 0-89228-102-2

JESUS, ALL IN ALL

"It flows . . . It challenges . . . It communicates the Gospel . . . It's Anne White's best book so far"—The Rev. Alva H. Brock Sr. Pastor, First United Methodist Church, Zephyrhills, Florida.

ANNE S. WHITE has given over 25 years of her life to a lay ministry of writing, counseling, teaching, speaking, and sharing Christ in churches of many denominations. Her extensive preparation and experience in the work of "Prayer Counseling" and other ministry have fitted her to write with authority. As an ecumenical Episcopalian, Mrs. White rejoices at the opportunity to work with all fellow Christians who are carrying out our Lord's Commission to His early disciples: "observe all that I have commanded you. . . ." Her emphasis is on the need for healing of relationships, of sick minds, emotions, spirits and bodies so that men may become whole in deeper commitment to Jesus Christ—their Lord, Savior, Redeemer, Healer, and Baptizer. Many have found healing as they read her books.

Since June 1972, the Lord has guided and provided for her to take clergy and lay teams with her to minister in England, Sweden, Finland, Holland, Australia, Manila, Kuala Lumpur, Singapore, and Canada—to set up Clergy Schools of Prayer Counseling and/or Missions and Retreats. She has spoken along with other outstanding leaders at many large annual Renewal Conferences in England and Australia as well as in the USA—including regional Episcopal Charismatic Fellowship Conferences and Women's Aglow International Conferences. In the course of this extended ministry, she has circled the globe nine times. All income from her lay ministry subsidizes Prayer Counseling Schools in the USA and abroad.

$3.95 plus postage.   ISBN 0-9605178-0-4

VICTORIOUS MINISTRY THROUGH CHRIST, INC.
P.O. BOX 1804 • WINTER PARK, FLORIDA 32790 • 407-657-4893

DAYSPRING
A Book of Prophecies and Scriptures

Meaningful for Today!
Originally published by LOGOS

    The Master speaks to His disciples through the Word of God and through the inspiration of His Holy Spirit. He illumines our minds and encourages us through prophecies, through the word of Wisdom and the word of Knowledge. Some of these writings were given by Him to this listener early one morning as she entered into a particularly difficult chapter of life. They have been tested and found helpful in the laboratory of her life. They are shared with the prayer that others too may find strength for the day as they pause each morning to meditate on the selected Scriptures and to listen for the Voice of the Master through these prophecies. He teaches, He comforts, He strengthens, He guides, He exhorts His disciples today—"forthtelling His Good News."

    "Anne White is one of the few who have learned to listen as well as to speak to God, and this has proved of great importance in her gifted healing ministry. She has also learned how to listen to people. . . . Prophecy should always be judged by scripture. But God *does* speak today through prophecies—as He did in the days of the apostles—always confirming, never contradicting the scriptures. I hope that many will use these readings and prophecies—one for each day of the year—in addition to their regular devotional habits; and that they will not limit the Holy Spirit, but expect Him to speak to them in ways additional to these written prophecies. Above all else I trust this book will teach us all to be better *listeners*. I believe it will.". . . **The Rev. Michael Harper, Fountain Trust, London, England.**

$4.95 plus postage

VICTORIOUS MINISTRY THROUGH CHRIST, INC.
P.O. BOX 1804 • WINTER PARK, FLORIDA 32790 • 407-657-4893

HEALING DEVOTIONS

A Revised edition, By Anne S. White

Published by Morehouse Barlow
A Sequel to HEALING ADVENTURE

This book may appeal to you because it is different from most devotional books. It is charismatic in every sense and will stimulate your understanding in respect to your own deepest needs and problems. It will help you to grow in faith as the Scriptures used become alive to you. And the simple prayers in "non-Churchy" language will encourage you to pray more spontaneously with new reality.

"The reading of HEALING DEVOTIONS has set my spirit singing and has given me new insights into God's power and will to heal today. I predict that, like Anne White's other books, God will use this one to bring restoration of the healing ministry to today's Church. To read it daily (with Scripture and hymnbook in hand) will, I believe, lead you toward greater 'wholeness' in Christ. . . . May the Holy Spirit use it to bring you deeper healing and guide you in your commitment to Jesus. May the gifts of the Spirit be lavished upon you, the fruit of the Spirit be in you, and may you go on from victory to victory with a 'singing faith'"
— The Rev. Alva H. Brock, Senior Pastor, First United Methodist Church, Zephyrills, Florida.

$4.95 plus postage   ISBN 8192-1192-3

Order from:
IMPACT BOOKS
137 W. Jefferson • Kirkwood, MO 63122

OR:
VICTORIOUS MINISTRY THROUGH CHRIST, INC.
P.O. BOX 1804 • WINTER PARK, FLORIDA 32790 • 407-657-4893

THE TRANSFORMING POWER OF GOD

An Old Favorite by Anne S. White

Anne S. White writes from a background of having proven what she says about the power of God to transform your life, to rid you of fears and futility and to enable you to live the life that is sure in faith, rich with the power of prayer, radiant with the known Presence of God, and powered with an eternal purpose.

Here is a book that is filled with vital anecdotes, practical suggestions and methods and rich spiritual interpretations. Learn from it:

- What is religion and what is Christianity
- Why Study the Bible and how to go about it
- How to experience the Presence of God
- What is Faith and how it can transform your life
- The power and method of true prayer
- How to conquer fear
- How to use Affirmations
- The effective use of Thanksgiving
- Stewardship, Self-Dedication and Purpose
- The Secret of Real Living
- How Christ Heals Today

$1.50 plus postage

VICTORIOUS MINISTRY THROUGH CHRIST, INC.
P.O. BOX 1804 • WINTER PARK, FLORIDA 32790 • 407-657-4893

TO ORDER BOOKS
by ANNE S. WHITE

send your order with a check or money order including postage to:

VICTORIOUS MINISTRY THROUGH CHRIST, INC.
POST OFFICE BOX 1804
WINTER PARK, FLORIDA 32790
407-657-4893

HEALING ADVENTURE --------------------*$4.95*

TRIAL BY FIRE-----------------------------*3.50*

Study Adventure in TRIAL BY FIRE-------------*1.95*

DAYSPRING--------------------------------*4.95*

TRANSFORMING POWER OF GOD------------*1.50*

JESUS, ALL IN ALL -----------------------*3.95*

FREED TO LIVE ---------------------------*4.95*

HEALING DEVOTIONS ---------------------*4.95*

POSTAGE FOR BOOK ORDERS:
1-2 books — $1.50, 3-5 books — $2.50,
6-9 books — $3.00, 10-15 books — $4.00

DISCOUNTS AVAILABLE FOR QUANTITY ORDERS.